**BAZILLION POINTS and
EERIE THINGS present...**

The Photography of
EERIE VON *(1981-2009)*

MISERY OBSCURA

Photographs and stories by EERIE VON
Art direction, design, and layout by TOM BEJGROWICZ
Content edited by EERIE VON & TOM BEJGROWICZ
Project coordinated for the author by
TOM BEJGROWICZ *with* RYAN J. DOWNEY

Contributing Photography by JAYE S. CLARKE, ROY AKIYAMA,
TED DOMURAT, LINGUINE, TOM BEJGROWICZ, & MORE where credited
Additional memorabilia supplied by JAYE S. CLARKE

BAZILLION POINTS | NEW YORK

*(front cover):
Eerie Von, May 1985
Photographic assistance by Mike Vayenas*

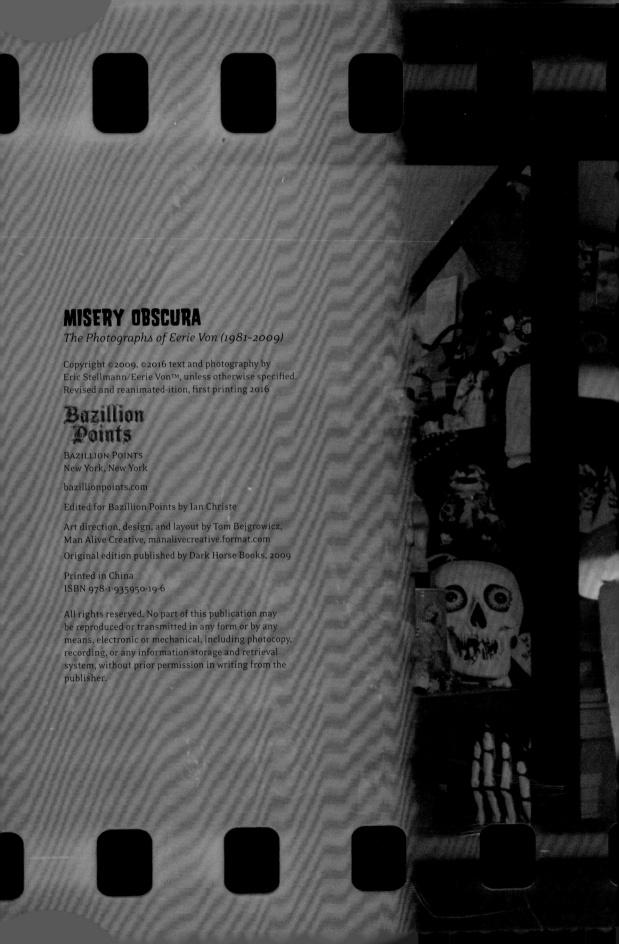

MISERY OBSCURA

The Photographs of Eerie Von (1981-2009)

Bazillion Points

BAZILLION POINTS
New York, New York

bazillionpoints.com

Edited for Bazillion Points by Ian Christe

Art direction, design, and layout by Tom Bejgrowicz,
Man Alive Creative, manalivecreative.format.com

Original edition published by Dark Horse Books, 2009

Printed in China
ISBN 978-1-935950-19-6

CONTENTS

5. Introduction: A 25-Year Document
by EERIE VON

6. Forewords: A Rite of Passage & From The Ashes
MIKE D'ANTONIO *and* LYLE PRESLAR

9. Chapter 1: Punk Rock High
THE MISFITS *and* ROSEMARY'S BABIES (1981-1982)

69. Chapter 2: All Murder, All Guts
SAMHAIN (1983-1987)

97. Chapter 3: At The Top Of The World
DANZIG (1987-1995)

157. Chapter 4: And Then There Was One...
SOLO WORK *and* FIEND ART (1995-2009)

This BOOK *is* A 25-YEAR DOCUMENT

of my life, both behind and in front of the camera. This is a photographic journal of the bands I was involved with, as well as the people I met, became friends with, and loved. While it is intended to reflect all of this first and foremost, it also serves as a scrapbook for a musical era. Those who were there—as well as those who wish they had been—can look on it and enjoy the images and memories evoked here. This has been a great rollercoaster ride, and I have loved every single minute—warts and all.

THANKS TO: TOM BEJGROWICZ; a talented man and a great friend, whose energy and determination made this book possible...RYAN DOWNEY, for his belief in this project and for getting my foot in the door...JEREMY ATKINS, MIKE RICHARDSON, and CHRIS WARNER at DARK HORSE for putting the ink to paper in 2009...JAYE CLARKE, for being there then and helping out now...The fans who shot us when I couldn't, because I was onstage, and sent us their pictures...My assistants who clicked the shutter when I couldn't (or simply because I wanted to be in the frame once in a while!)...And everyone to whom I handed my camera in order to help capture a moment—family, friends, crew guys, and girlfriends. I thank you all for helping contribute to this book.

MISERY OBSCURA IS DEDICATED TO: The fans, our families, and friends who always supported us in ROSEMARY'S BABIES, THE MISFITS, SAMHAIN, and DANZIG...THE RAMONES, without whom none of us would be who we are, and all the bands that came before them... Those we have loved and lost, whose memory we will continue to honor...And especially to those who carry the torch of doing their own thing, forever aspiring to create something new and brilliant. As long as kids with guitars are getting together in somebody's basement, all will be right with the world. Every once in a while, something great happens...

A RITE OF PASSAGE

FOREWORD *by* MIKE D'ANTONIO

I remember seeing Metallica sporting Misfits shirts and tattoos back in the day. I knew from the imagery that I *needed* to hear what this band was about. Once I did, the Misfits and Samhain changed my life forever. Starting at age fourteen with *Legacy Of Brutality* (the second LP I ever owned), I could not get enough. Suddenly, I was wearing black clothes and sporting a Devilock haircut. Nothing could tame my need for Glenn Danzig's dark horror lyrics and creep-tastic sing-alongs. Suddenly the Crimson Ghost was all over my school books and on the grip tape of my skateboard. Singing about *hacking the heads off little girls and putting them on my wall* while walking to my high school locker became a daily ritual! That Misfits infatuation lasted until I heard Samhain, a band that instantly became a classic in my world. Samhain was more evil, and even better musically then the Misfits had hoped to be. Nothing could match the creepy, almost gothic, Samhain guitar leads. I ate, slept, and dreamed the artwork and the music. I remember how much the *Initium* album cover freaked out my parents—and I loved it. After they were so bothered by the imagery, I became hell-bent on wallpapering my bedroom with the blood-soaked band photos. And so I did. ■ Thinking back to the old days, I can say beyond a shadow of a doubt that the Samhain and Danzig bass playing gave me the craving to start playing music. Ominous, yet simple and to-the-point, Eerie Von's solid, driving bass encouraged me towards a similar straightforward, no-nonsense way of playing. As a matter of fact, the day after I bought my first bass, I called a friend to teach me how to play. He asked what I wanted to learn, and I demanded only Misfits and Samhain songs. They were quite easy to learn, yet so fun to play, even to this day. ■ When Danzig's first album came out, everything changed again. Finally, Danzig had hired a qualified drummer! What a change, what a sound; the next level had come again—but with overtones of Led Zeppelin? Well, you can't win 'em all, but at least the music was played well. The gatefold vinyl jacket of the giant Danzig skull still hangs on my wall. It's impressive. I remember being excited, yet, at the same time, bummed for that album's commercial success. Back then, it was cooler to keep bands like this to oneself; keep it underground. Essentially, Danzig brought heavier, more evil, metal music to the mainstream, and inevitably opened doors into pop culture for many bands, including mine, Killswitch Engage. ■ Visually, I have always tried to emulate the stark contrasts of the Misfits and Samhain/Danzig skulls, and their powerful, simplistic imagery. These designs encapsulate the ideal visual logo, equipped with a fine blend of corporate branding and DIY ethics. The album artwork spoke to me, and demanded my attention. How could anyone *not* fall in love with Pushead's psychotic "Evil Eye" design? Like joining a cult, wearing a Misfits, Samhain, or Danzig shirt was a rite of passage into an exclusive, underground "Fiend Club." And like I said, if it bothered my parents, I was *all about it*. ■ For myself and many others in bands on the road, this book is easy to relate to. The dirty venues, the vans, and the DIY attitude are all here. These things make us stronger away from home. Starting from the bottom and learning the ropes as I went was the only way I knew. We had nothing to rely on but our fellow band members, and no goal except to get to the next gig. I have lived this stuff, but only after the Misfits, Samhain, and Danzig paved the way. Touring has not gotten any easier, but maybe the rough spots have become more expected as a band rises through the ranks. ■ From graphic design to music, the Misfits, Samhain, and Danzig have all warped me into the person I am today. I am forever addicted to the dark, in love with horror, and always ready for a sing-along chorus. I can't imagine a world without these bands, and I know for a fact that my bands Overcast and Killswitch Engage would never have existed without them.

(above):
Photograph by Kenny Gabor

In addition to being the guitarist and founding member of the godly Minor Threat,
Lyle Preslar was also in the Initium-*era lineup of Samhain. He tracked guitars and*
worked on material for the album, but we parted ways well before Initium *saw the light*
of day. Prior to things falling apart, we played one show together —Samhain's first-ever
show— on March 31, 1984, at the infamous Rock Hotel in New York. The posters for billed
*us appropriately: "From the ashes of the Misfits and Minor Threat...*SAMHAIN.*" Just*
like that, I was onstage surrounded by punk rock royalty. I will always remember that
moment. While our memories of the night may differ, I'm thrilled to be forever linked
with one of my musical heroes.

FROM THE ASHES

ROCK HOTEL $1

FOREWORD *by* LYLE PRESLAR

I had freshly fallen off the harDCore bandwagon when I got on the Amtrak train to New York City to perform the first Samhain show. The venue, Rock Hotel, was a downtown joint that seemed to be run by a small, screwy basehead with massive armed henchmen, as I would sadly discover at a later date. The band had some rehearsals, and we had recorded what I think is a great album in a studio in some New Jersey suburb. My post-Minor Threat world was revolving around a friendly sun. ■ Nonetheless, I was plagued by nearly seizure-inducing fears. If Mr. Danzig proved to be as generally sticky as he had over the last several months (e.g., that incident in the A&P supermarket checkout aisle that the federal authorities had been made aware of), I might have to kill him—onstage, if necessary, for the safety of the crowd. If the rest of the Samhain posse proved as musically porous as they had demonstrated in the studio, Danzig's grave in the Pine Barrens' would have to include them, as well. Yet, being enthusiastically versed in all types of musical combat, I courageously sallied forth via the U.S. rail system from D.C.'s Union Station. In tow and armed to the teeth were my trusty comrades Brian Baker (punk rock's greatest bass player, and, as it would turn out, one of its finest guitar gods) and my gal friend at the time, Maria. ■ The sound check on that early spring evening was the stuff of rock star nightmares. Glenn was sick with a chest cold (nix that golden voice), and the band was as bad as ever. To make matters more dire, my one request—a Marshall JCM stack for my Gibson gitbox—was missing from the rented, SIR-supplied backline. Instead, what did we behold, but a matching set of Fender Twins! Brian wanted to incinerate them, and it took everything that I could do to prevent his malicious arsonous intent, including obtaining an off-session judicial restraining order. Fortunately, we were close to the courthouse. Still, I agreed with him—they sounded like absolute pig shit. Of course, I had brought an MXR fuzz pedal with my Les Paul. That would have to do. On the bright side, at least the band appeared to be gloriously lacking in arm bands and eye makeup! As was our understanding, Samhain was not to be the Misfits II. I marched about in my field dress: a gray Minor Threat sweatshirt that you would kill to sell on eBay today. I looked ridiculous, so I turned it inside out—and looked even more ridiculous. ■

Après sound check, Maria, Brian, and I went for dinner at some lower, lower West Side Herzegovinan steakhouse/sushi/goulash spot. We felt relatively secure that the situation was salvageable. Glenn would have a couple of cough drops; there would be no reprise of the 'Fits couture cartoon horror splendor; and the Fender Twins would deliver enough righteous fuzzbox noise to drown out the rest of the shit. In short, Samhain would rule. ■ Then imagine this: I returned to the friendly backstage confines of the Rock Hotel, only to find my bandmates in *full-on 'Fits Devilock mode.* Jesus, Eerie had on a fuckin' homemade *black* Spiderman outfit (decades before the most recent movies). The hairspray was so thick and bilious that the fire marshal phoned up for a preemptive bribe. (This was '80s New York, after all.) I was in serious wardrobe trouble, and on the verge of total panic. But I had saved the day by packing a black T-shirt to go with my black Levi's. Hey, ho—let's go! ■ I remember little about the performance, other than knowing we sucked before a modest crowd. The Damned were likely playing across town, with Brian and Maria in attendance, for all I knew. During the ensuing rail return to D.C., my compatriots confirmed this grim assessment. (God, I wish we had the good sense to do drugs!) So, judging from my memory of that night's music, and looking at the contents of this book, Eerie would probably have been better off sans Spiderman getup and avec camera. And today I would have some good shots of my T-shirt and jeans framed next to Mssr. Danzig. ■ The duds notwithstanding, Eerie Von was the only voice of reason in Samhain. He tried to calm the turbulent waters left in the wake of the super-warship egos belonging to Glenn and me. I'm just sorry that he couldn't save the Bauhaus-influenced guitar parts I recorded for *Initium* (or at least a tape of them). If he had been the boss, I might have stayed on the job with him, and been content as a fat-ass rock star. Over the years, I noted his musical success—he got a *lot* better during his stints in Samhain and the staggering juggernaut that was Danzig—although ultimately I think much more of him as a photographic artist. Dear reader, I will bet a "From the Ashes of..." poster (which I don't actually have) that you will find this book offers all the necessary testimony to his tremendous eye.

LODI HIGH SCHOOL

LODI, N.J.

chapter 1

PUNK rOck HiGh '78 - '82

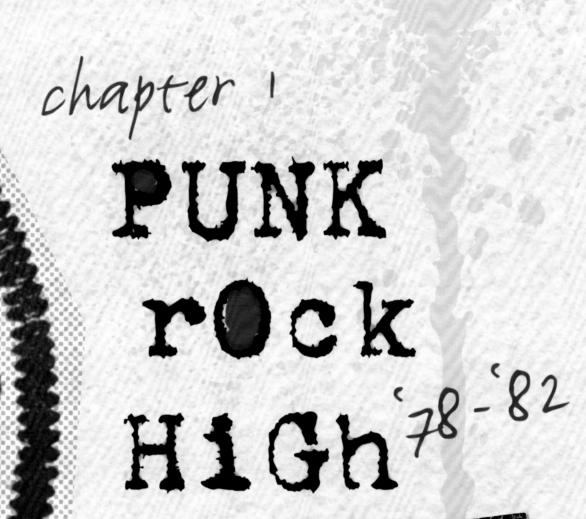

I never wanted Lodi High School to end. For three of my four years, I took pictures, made T-shirts, and hung out with Doyle—it was a blast. The modification of this school postcard (above) was done by Mr. "A," our beloved art teacher. He knew I would have stayed in high school if I could have.

LODI HIGH SCHOOL

LODI, NEW JERSEY

Approved by the Department of Pu[blic] Instruction, State of New Jersey, and ac[credited] as a member of the Middle State[s] Association of Colleges and Secondary Schools.

REPORT CARD

of

Name *Stellmann, Eric*

Home Room *11-7* Class *211*

Home Room Teacher *Mrs. Thompso[n]*

19 *80* 19 *81*

NONAN

LEFT TO RIGHT
GRAIG RICHARDSON, STEVE BLACKBURN, JOHN BARDINO, PAUL GAWIN
BERNIE GUARINO, ME, PETE NESTEROWITZ, JOHN VARGAS
~~PAUL VANHARNER~~ CHARLIE DESTAFANO + BOB STICA.

PHOTO TAKEN BY DIANE RUSSO

Mr Van Beveren	U.S Hist 2	**Mark**	B	B	A	D	C	B	5

(above)
This is the U.S. History 2 class of 1980-81, with Mr. Van. To the far left is Craig Richardson, who played guitar in my first band, Rosemary's Babies. Craig still plays, and continues to be a photographer, as well.

I'm the handsome devil in the middle with the wrist bands, trying to get John Vargass to stop laughing.

To my immediate right is Paul Gawin, a great drummer. He showed me Glenn's favorite beat when I wanted to try out for the Misfits. We took lessons at the local Boys Club as kids; the only difference was, he had talent.

(right)
Here's Doyle dressed in football uniform at the senior homecoming assembly. He provided some of his buddies on the team with the black wrist bands that the Misfits wore. The coaches hated that, and they would often make Doyle and I take them off. I was on the basketball team. [right] Seems silly now, doesn't it?

I'm a 16 year old punk, and my first photoshoot is...

August '81

can't remember exactly how or when Doyle asked me to take photos of the band, but it was quite informal. He simply asked, *Why don't you shoot the Misfits?* There seemed to be some miscommunication over the day and time, because I wasn't at home when the band came to get me for the shoot! It was either Saturday or Sunday, and I was where I spent most of my time—at Kennedy Park playing basketball. ■ The guys showed up in one of their many Chevy Blazers, driving over the grass right up to the fence that enclosed the basketball courts. They shouted, *What are you doing? You're supposed to be taking pictures today!* ■ I jumped on my bicycle and raced home, while the band attempted to run me off the road the entire way back to my house. Inside, I grabbed my Dad's camera—a Nikkormat, which my grandmother had brought back from Japan ten years earlier—plus my sister's Mamiya. I might have had film, as well, but seeing as how I didn't know we were supposed to shoot, I guess we could have stopped to buy film somewhere along the way. ■ I remember wearing sweats and

a T-shirt. I didn't change from the basketball court. I learned pretty fast that when the Misfits wanted to do something, that usually meant right now—so off we went. I met Glenn and Googy for the first time that day. Kenny, aka "Schlock"—Jerry Only and Doyle's brother, was driving the Blazer. I knew Kenny from school. He was a gifted sculptor, and a ball-buster. ■ Everyone knew where we were going, and it didn't matter that I had no idea. The cave where we were supposed to shoot was either in upstate New

York or Northern Jersey, I can't remember, but it took a while to get there. Except for vaguely remembering Googy rolling a joint on a drum head, I recall very little of the drive itself. I didn't partake in the smoking, was nervous enough already; how would I focus the camera if I had? ■ The cave, located in the woods where caves are found, was a party spot, surely visited before by Kenny, Jerry, and some of their friends. The weather was warm and dry, and we arrived early in the day, when the light was still good. I had managed to bring a flash for the Mamiya. I loaded it up with color film, set the shutter on 1/60th of a second, and varied the lens opening as I saw fit. This camera was mainly for backup; a novelty, really. I didn't think color film was appropriate for these guys, especially in a cave. ■ The meat of the shoot would be handled by my trusty Nikkormat, loaded with Tri-X Pan, 400 speed, black-and-white film. That was good for low light situations, which the day was sure to be, taking place in a cave and all. I proceeded to pretend I knew what I was doing while answering Glenn's questions about camera stuff. He had some experience with photography back in school, and had done most of the band's promo shoots in the past. There were some wardrobe adjustments, but, for the most part, these guys had been wearing their Misfits gear and makeup since leaving home earlier in the day. We were good to go. ■ I was freaking! Glenn told me to make sure and let them know when I was going to shoot. He was constantly fiddling with his hair. Getting Googy to pay attention was a bit of a chore, so I wound up counting to three or four on quite a number of occasions. ■ Jerry and Doyle were very easy to shoot. Even though Doyle had not been in the band long, he made good faces, and he knew how to look scary. Jerry was a pro. He always knew when the camera was on him, and always looked kool. ■ I had so many shots to choose from. *How about this?...How about here?...Oh, that looks kool...Gotta remember to focus...This might look good in color...Turn on the flash...Close the lens...Shit, Glenn wasn't looking...*
■ These guys looked kool even against a plain backdrop, so to have them in a cave with a bunch of jagged rocks and shadows was too good to be true. I would do anything to get a good shot or make something look more interesting. I was learning as I went along. I laid down on a pointy rock floor for what felt like forever, just to get a few exposures. ■ After a while, I thought that was enough in the caves, let's go outside and see what the camera says. The cave was up on a ridge, and there were lots of trees, valleys, places

to climb, and just so many possibilities. ■ I had to be ready, as I followed Doyle and Jerry to the next location. Jerry would stop and pose, and it would look kool, so I had to shoot it. Glenn kept telling me not to waste my film, so I didn't take as many candid shots to document the day as I should have. No one was concerned with remembering the shoot itself, the goal was just getting a few good shots of the band. At this point, I had no idea if these would be used, or if Glenn had something specific in mind; no one said anything. ■ I posed the band at the mouth of the cave, as if that was where they lived, or hung out when not on stage. The image made sense to me. We were getting good stuff. *Googy, look at the camera once in a while.* Why did he wear white pants? Why did I let him sit in front? His bleached blonde hair and white face reflected all the light. What a rookie mistake! I was sixteen, what did I know? I had just met these other two guys, I wasn't about to order them around. But how could he wear white? How come the other guys didn't tell him to wear black? ■ The four guys were posed up on a rock ledge, looking down at me. Jerry and Doyle crossed their arms in superhero poses. You could tell Jerry was a big influence on his "little" brother, who was probably six-two to his six feet. Glenn was much smaller, but he had a big personality and a good sense of humor. He was more relaxed in his poses, and seemed to take more risks— but the hair was constantly diverting his attention. He was the only one who brought a few different things to wear. ■ Jerry brought one of his basses; he never did a shoot without one. The bass had a lot of personality—it was a cut-up vintage Rickenbacker, molested nightly onstage, glued and electrical-taped back together with a plywood headstock and a plastic skull from Ken's Magic Shop in Clifton. The leather strap was adorned with large spikes, handmade by the brothers at their father's machine shop. ■ As we lost the light, we packed up the paper mâché skulls Glenn had carefully placed around the cave. We put on our leather jackets and headed back through the woods towards the Blazer. I only shot four rolls in all. How many good shots did I get? Any at all? What mistakes had I made? I hoped I didn't fuck up. You didn't get too many chances to make a good impression on Glenn. ■ I probably developed the film that very night. I'm sure I wouldn't have slept, otherwise. Out of the fixer and into the water, indeed. ■ Oh yeah—I got some good ones. *Oh man, look at these!* I had to buy paper, I couldn't wait to print them. *Gotta make a contact sheet for the guys.* ■ I did good. Kool.

(left) Later on in the '80s, when we were hanging out with Metallica, I made this shirt—featuring a "cave" photo of mine—for James Hetfield. I added glow-in-the-dark paint to the logo, and it was definitely one of a kind. Since those guys were big stars by that point, if they wore one of our shirts, millions of people would see it. Good way to get people talking, I figured. And it worked, eventually.

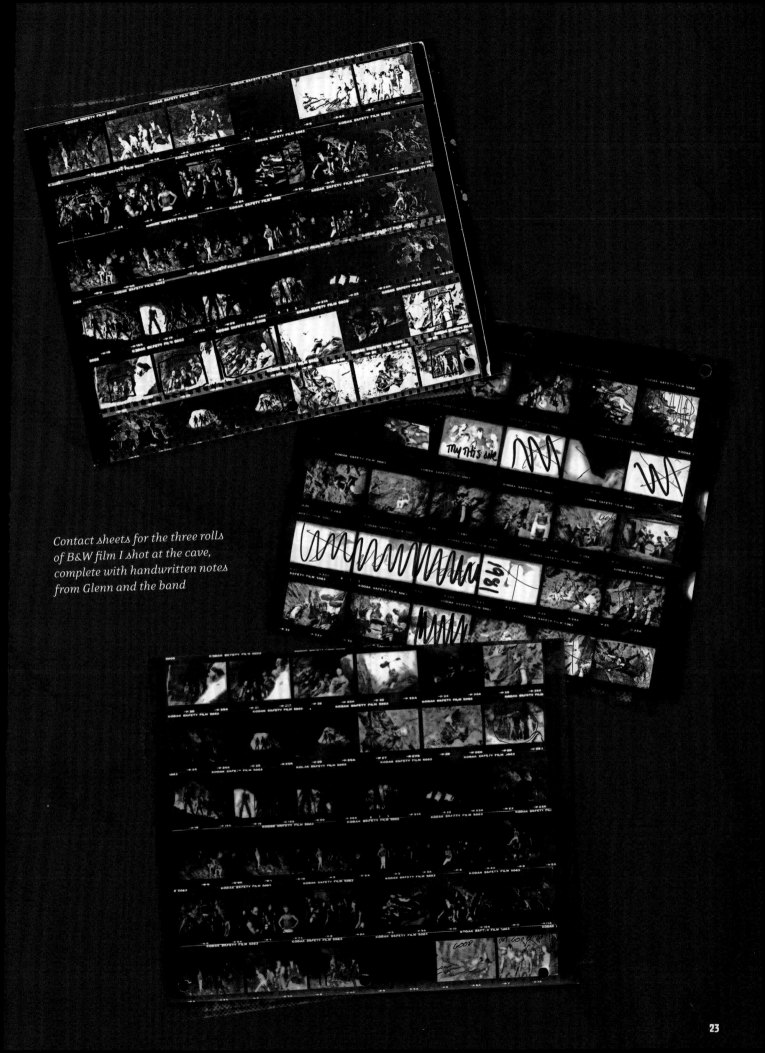

Contact sheets for the three rolls
of B&W film I shot at the cave,
complete with handwritten notes
from Glenn and the band

Chase Park. Aug. 15, '81

Chase Park was so named because the club was two floors above a Chase Manhattan Bank on Houston Street. I always loved going into the city. I started going there with my sister Sue when I was fourteen or so, to shop at thrift stores and eat at Mamoun's Falafel. My first show ever was the Misfits, on Halloween 1980 at Irving Plaza. I went as the Invisible Man. That was Doyle's first show in the band. For me, it was nice way to start a lifestyle. ■ Chase Park was my first chance to shoot the band live. Since I wasn't taking pictures before the show, I could help carry the coffins, couldn't I? Who made these things out of two-by-fours and plywood? They were really heavy, but the show was only on the third floor, and I was young and strong, *sort of.* A big black garbage can filled with Heineken and ice also had to go up those three flights. Where was Clayton Barker, our big black friend and Lodi High football star? He was there for security, and looked very inconspicuous. Days before the show, Doyle or Jerry had brought me the "Fiend Club" screen, and I printed up some shirts for the security team. They came out kind of gray; well, they got what they paid for. ■ On the way into the city, we slammed into the car in front of us, bending the frame of our car and causing the door not to shut. I can still see one of the wooden coffins, perched atop a Chevy Blazer, flying off into the distance. After the accident, with the door now permanently ajar, Doyle held it closed all the way into town. I was sure he would cramp up before show time, but I don't recall him having any trouble playing. ■ Chase Park was a decent room, with a stage two- or three-feet high, mirrors all over one wall, and plenty of room for the coffins. I took photos at the sound check. Glenn hated that. The band couldn't use any pictures from sound check; Doyle was wearing blue jeans, and he didn't have his Misfits face on! The big secret was that the band was going to do an Elvis song that night. Weeks before, I had lent Glenn a couple of Elvis records. He thought it would be fun to try "Whole Lotta Livin' To Do," from the *Loving You* soundtrack. ■ I took some pics of the guys putting on makeup, and discussed the Elvis song with Glenn. He had the words on a small piece of paper, and we debated who had the right lyrics. Being a huge Elvis fan, I was sure that I was right, while Glenn, being Glenn, was sure that I was wrong. It didn't matter much, really. ■ One a.m. rolled around, and the Misfits were still not onstage. I tried very hard not to take pictures. Friends from Lodi High dropped by the dressing room to have a beer. The band had brought a bunch of the posters for *3 Hits From Hell*, The crew guys taped two of them together, wrote a set list in giant letters, and taped it to the floor. I believe the band took the stage at three a.m. That wasn't unusual for a punk rock show in the city, by the way. Googy had on black pajamas, and he had recently shaved his head. The coffins were set up. *Here we go!* ■ Everything was completely dark except for a few colored lights. I couldn't focus, because I couldn't see. I tried to use the flash, but that didn't really help with the focus problem. I just had to wing it. I made many mistakes at this first show, but still managed to get a few good shots. I learned that Glenn didn't like profile shots, Jerry was constantly moving, and Doyle liked to stand still. Doyle was wearing his first pair of arm bands. In school the week before, he and I printed a small Crimson Ghost head on fake white leather. He painted a red circle around it, and attached it to two wristbands sewn together. It looked pretty kool. He was also wearing the shirt from the cave shoot. ■ I don't remember what songs they played. I missed a lot, just looking through the lens. The Elvis song came off well, although only Glenn and I appreciated it. Nobody else knew what it was. I can still see the little jump move that Jerry and Doyle did at one spot in the tune. When you think about it now; Glenn singing an Elvis song in the Misfits is pretty damn kool. I don't think they ever did that song again. ■ The show wasn't long. Afterwards, seriously cold beer and congratulations were given all around, as fans and friends came backstage to pay their respects. We hung around for a while. I took more photos and had some beer. I was beginning to like this world. I would like to be in this band. Maybe I could kill Googy...

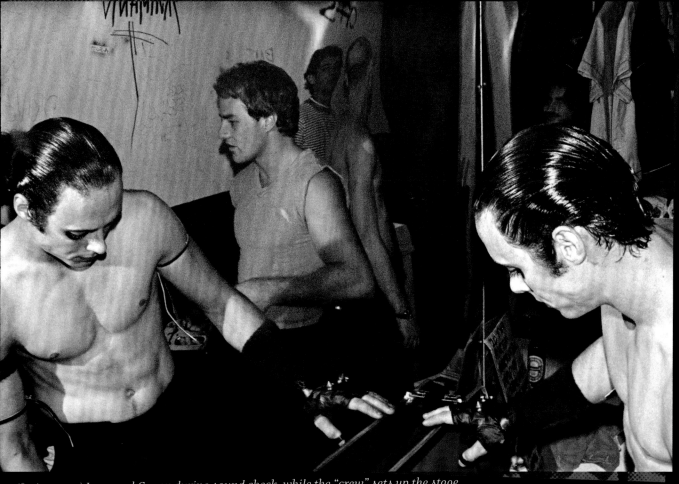

(facing page) Jerry and Googy during sound check, while the "crew" sets up the stage
(this page) Doyle and Jerry apply their makeup before the show. (below) Glenn is in the back, and that's Yvette, Doyle's girl.

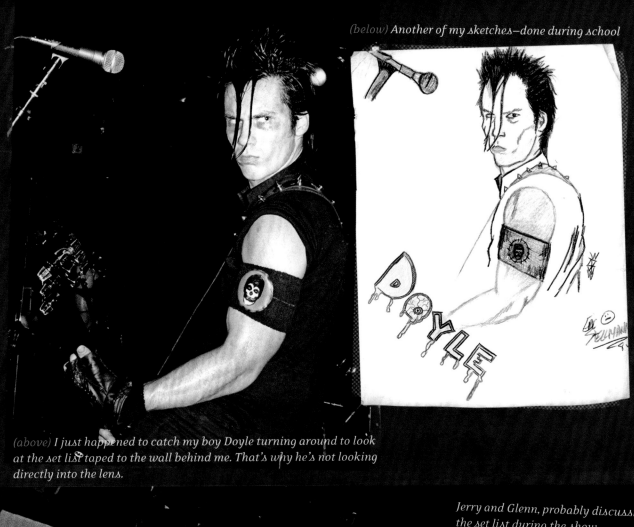

(below) Another of my sketches—done during school

(above) I just happened to catch my boy Doyle turning around to look at the set list taped to the wall behind me. That's why he's not looking directly into the lens.

Jerry and Glenn, probably discussing the set list during the show

Jerry and Annette; She was a local scene-maker, who owned a record store around St. Mark's Place called Free Being. I used to go there all the time. There was a Static Age poster from way back up on the ceiling.

Rum & Coke was Glenn's drink of choice back then, so that's probably what he's drinking, while Doyle sucks on an ice cube.

Clockwise from top left: Pepe (roadie friend from the city); Eerie Von; Jerry Only; Clayton Barker (friend from Lodi High), Glenn, and Doyle. Photo taken by Ken Caiafa, with my sister's Mamiya.

Glenn is talking with Annette, who just told him how great he was tonight. The band was promoting the 3 Hits From Hell EP, and during the show had handed out posters like the one behind him.

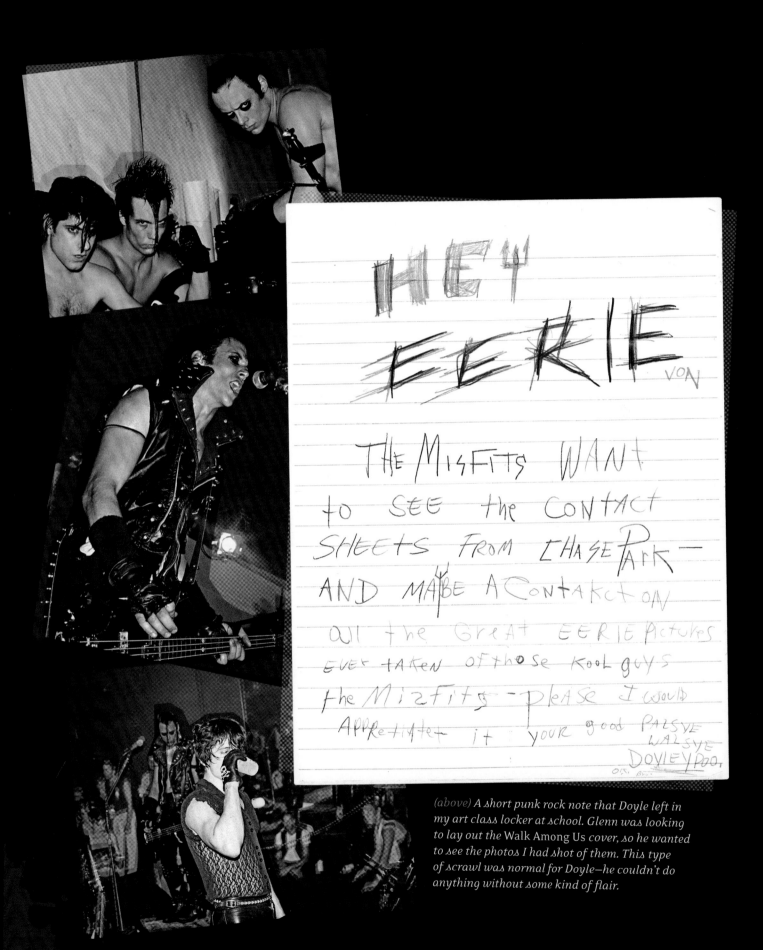

HEY

EERIE VON

THE MISFITS WANT
to SEE the CONTACT
SHEETS FROM CHASE PARK—
AND MAYBE A CONTAKCT ON
all the GREAT EERIE Pictures
ever taken of those kool guys
the Misfits—please I would
APPReTiATe+ it your good PALSYE
WALSYE
DOYLEYPoo,

(above) A short punk rock note that Doyle left in
my art class locker at school. Glenn was looking
to lay out the Walk Among Us cover, so he wanted
to see the photos I had shot of them. This type
of scrawl was normal for Doyle—he couldn't do
anything without some kind of flair.

Philadelphia is only an hour-and-a-half away from Lodi, New Jersey. When the Misfits were booked to play the East Side Club in August of 1981, I was invited along to hang, shoot the band, and witness the devastation. I don't recall how we got there; I'm sure one of the Chevy Blazers went and maybe a van with equipment. The coffins the band used on stage stayed home for this gig. This was my second time shooting the band live, so I was eager to correct the mistakes I had made the first time. Once again, I brought two cameras; one loaded one with color film and the other B&W. ■ I made the first of my color *Horror Business* T-shirts a few days before, and Doyle wound up wearing it on stage. That was

band as if I was capturing a sporting event. I would position myself in a place where the action would come to me. I learned how the band moved, and what patterns they were likely to repeat. Jerry moved the most, so I would focus on a spot, and wait for him to run into the frame. Doyle didn't move much back then. He simply pounded that Ibanez guitar into submission; down-strumming so fast that his whole forearm was a blur. Incredible. ■ Glenn had smaller movements at this time; his intensity was all on his face. He didn't thrash around as much as he would later. He didn't have to. That voice didn't need a big show to complement it. I tried to shoot Googy a little more than I had the first time around,

a proud moment for me, I must admit. Glenn had done a black-and-white version, but I didn't know that at the time. My shirts were painstakingly hand-painted, each and every one. I didn't have the setup for multiple screens, so I just printed the black ink on white cotton and filled in the rest. I wanted to proudly walk around wearing one of the coolest record covers ever. Glenn complained about the quality of the cover art; he used to call it "Blurry Business," but of course I had to have one. ■ The East Side Club wasn't large, and the gig was intimate. Other friends were also invited along to join in on the fun. Every outing seemed more like a happening rather than just a show. I think the band liked that gang mentality—the more, the merrier! I know that's the vibe Jerry gave off then, and still does now. ■ This is where I learned to shoot the

but every shot I got looked the same. I did manage a few backstage shots before the show, but the band was never big on these so I didn't "waste" too many exposures. There never seemed to be enough time to properly shoot these guys, everything was always over so fast. Again, I didn't really get to watch the show. I figured I was there to do my thing, so I did it. I would have to remember what I could about the show through the photos I took. ■ There had been some beers before the gig, but no food. So, on the way home after the show, after the gear was packed up, we went to McDonald's and celebrated another Misfits victory with a cheeseburger or two. I didn't get home until early in the morning, falling asleep with my boots on. When it was time for school in the morning, Mom asked me if I had any tests. When I replied *no*, she let me go back to sleep. Awesome!!!

Doyle stands alone in the doorway of the
dressing room, moments before the attack.
I just happened to turn around to catch that
Devilock in a perfect silhouette.

Jerry wanting to take a bite out of the thigh of his then-girlfriend, Linda, who eventually became Mrs. Only.

Doyle wearing my Horror Business *shirt and one of Jerry's old studded collars*

Glenn shows off his now-famous bone gloves. Today, you can't be in a horror rock band without a pair. He painted these himself, because you weren't likely to find them on the shelf. On occasion, he was known to give them away to close friends at the end of tours.

(this page) Glenn feeds "Mr. Garbage Can." I later included this shot in the collage on the Rosemary's Babies EP. Glenn was always joking around like this back then.

(above) A flyer for a show with the Necros in Detroit on 9/12/81, only a couple weeks after the East Side Club show.

(above) I wasn't always "eerie," but I was always EERIE VON.

(below) This might have been for class; Me shooting Doyle, him shooting me.

(above) This is the way we looked during our senior year at Lodi High. We were still wearing colors. I'm trying to look kool while Doyle clowns around, as usual. Photo by Mr. A.

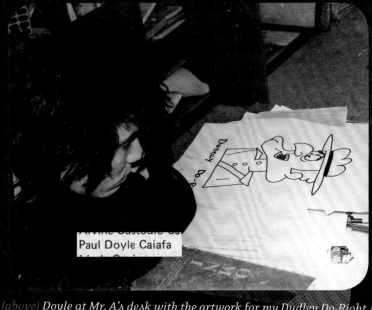

Paul Doyle Caiafa

(above) Doyle at Mr. A's desk with the artwork for my Dudley Do-Right shirt.

(left) This is Yvette, Doyle's girlfriend during senior year. She was the only hot, spooky chick in school, and I had a big crush on her. Maybe I could kill Doyle...

CLASS OF 1982

(above) Mom and Dad were so proud.

Eric Von Stellmann

Benson Bruce Benjamin

Some of our friends came to see us graduate. No one could believe it! That's JR from Rosemary's Babies in the red shirt.

I borrowed a cape and Bruce and I shaved our heads, just to piss people off.

The Misfits at Irving Plaza—those very words take me back. I spent a lot of time at the club at Irving Place and East 15th back in the early 1980s. Some serious shows happened there: national acts with local talent opening, three or more bands per bill for ten bucks or less. I saw my first show ever at the Irving: the Misfits on Halloween 1980. I love that place. ■ This was supposed to be my first gig as drummer with the band. A month earlier, I had tried out and gotten the job. Glenn said they had a show a month away. That was on a Friday—but by Monday I had decided not to join. See, I was in the middle of doing my own band, putting out my first record, and I didn't wanna give all that up just to play drums (and shut up), even if it was for the Misfits. Seeing how things worked out, I don't regret my decision one bit. ■ The Necros came from the Midwest to play, too, and Todd Swalla, their amazing drummer, was enlisted to sit in for the night. He had done that before for the Misfits. There were no hard feelings, so I went along to shoot the show. I only got a couple shots of the Necros. I didn't shoot the opening band, which might have been the Beastie Boys, or Heart Attack—with a sixteen-year-old Jesse Malin. I forget. ■ Doyle and Kenny were wearing Star Trek shirts, and Glenn had a freshly-screened Count Chocula shirt for the occasion. He told me to make sure I got the first three songs, because after that, "we look a mess." Irving Plaza held about a thousand on a good night, and the Misfits always packed in a crowd. The stage was small, but the room was good, with a great vibe from hosting all the greats throughout the punk and hardcore days. Our band Danzig even did a show there, for a freakin' dollar, after appearing on THE JON STEWART SHOW in 1994. I was happy to be on that stage again, for sure. ■ This night I would spend either in the pit or on the stage, fighting the crowd to get my shots and watching my friends kick ass onstage. The band was really hot, and the crowd loved them. Glenn got down on the stage, right in the crowd. People would be stage diving, kicking him in the head, jumping on him, trying to scream into the mic. He really took a beating, and always came back for more. A massive slam circle formed, as it usually did, and bodies flailed and churned like meat in a food processor. Jerry worked the stage back and forth and side to side, whipping the bass around, nearly taking Glenn's head off a few times. Glenn had taken a few whacks from Jerry's bass over the years, but tonight he was lucky. ■ Doyle had a mic on his side of the stage for backing vocals. He did manage to contribute a few times at this show. Soon after he gave up singing to concentrate on being Frankenstein with guitar. He was in rare form at Irving Plaza, breaking almost every string on his guitar before the curtain came down. ■ I probably shot three rolls of thirty-six-exposure B&W film with a flash while documenting the evening. I got a lot of good stuff, one frame at a time. I had no motor drive; I had to shoot until I got a good one, and then I would move on. The band had yet to develop the two-hour show, where they did every song they knew before going home, so the night was over in a flash (probably a little more than an hour). After all, the 'Fits put everything they had into it, and couldn't keep it up for too long. ■ The Misfits at Irving Plaza. If only...

(left) *This is one of my all-time favorite shots of Glenn; it shows the intensity he put into every song. I was fighting off people in the pit for this shot.*

(above) Before the show, Glenn shows off the new Count Chocula shirt he made.
(below) Minutes before taking the stage, Doyle gives me the Vulcan salute.

(above) I love shots of the crowd. The band shirts you see people wearing at this show are classic: Dead Kennedys, Bad Brains, Black Flag, and more

(below) I know from experience that Glenn is asking the monitor man why he can't hear himself. Maybe it's because Jerry and Doyle have a wall of amps all turned up to 10. Maybe. Just maybe.

Jerry treating his bass with no respect at all. See the heaps of electrical tape holding that thing together?

(below) I was trying to capture what it really felt like to be at a Misfits show. Here's Doyle letting the fans play his guitar; the idea seemed to go over quite well.

(above) *Todd Swalla, drummer for the Necros; he filled in on drums for the Misfits a few times over the years.*

(above) *The Necros, shot from the balcony; (from left) Corey, Todd, Barry and Brian.*

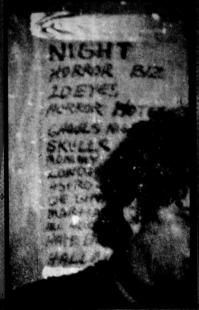

(left) This detail shows one of set lists taped up around the stage at Irving Plaza. Did punk rock get any better than this?

1. Night of the Living Dead
2. Horror Business
3. 20 Eyes
4. Horror Hotel
5. Ghouls Night Out
6. Skulls
7. Mommy, Can I Go Out And Kill Tonight?
8. London Dungeon
9. Astro Zombies
10. We Are 138
11. I Turned Into a Martian
12. All Hell Breaks Loose
13. Hatebreeders
14. Halloween

Jersey City, New Jersey; I went to this show primarily to see Gang Green from Boston. Both Glenn and I were really into them that summer. The *This Is Boston, Not L.A.* record was all we were listening to. While he and I were getting to be better friends, I was hanging out less and less with Jerry and Doyle. I had met the new drummer, Robo, since he was living with Glenn at the time. This was the first show I had seen with him on drums. ■ I was doing my band, Rosemary's Babies, at the time, while working midnights at a chemical plant and hoping to raise enough money to put out a record. Overall, I was less involved with the Misfits than I had been a few months earlier. ■ I picked Glenn's brain about band stuff and music in general. He gave me advice and all the phone numbers he had, and he pretty much told me how to go about pressing your own record. It would have been much harder to find all this out on my own, and I really appreciated his help. From our many conversations, I began to see where the Misfits were heading, and what Glenn really wanted in a band. We agreed on a lot of things when it came to music, our objectives, and how things should be done within a band. ■ Rosemary's Babies was still pretty much a three-piece at the time. We were starting to write better songs, while getting to be a tight little unit. Next step was the recording studio, but first we still needed a singer.

Some time later, this photo was used for the infamous Evilive "3-pack." When Glenn decided to do a second pressing of the Fiend Club-only Evilive EP, he ended up with extra records with no sleeves, so he came up with the 3-pack idea, packing the remainders in sets with three different covers featuring the band members. I was very happy he chose one of my photos for his cover. Last I heard, a 3-pack went for $10,000.

While I was waiting around for the Misfits to again require the services of a new drummer, I practiced a lot and began to write the words that would eventually become songs for my first band, Rosemary's Babies. We were just Bob and I at first, trying to decide what kind of band we wanted to be, looking for a name and thumbing through horror mags—one after another—until I came upon an article about *Rosemary's Baby*. That rang my bell. That was a kool film, and would be a good name. Bob dug it as well. ■ Bob knew this guy, Craig, that lived nearby and played guitar. I knew him, too; he was in some of my classes, and he was a photographer like me, but I didn't know he played. Turns out Craig was into the Ramones—that was good enough for me. Plus he lived near Bob, so I figured they could come to rehearsal together. Now we were cookin'! ■ Bob and I were both pissed off about working at jobs we hated; he worked at a local grocery store, and I was stuck at a chemical plant. We saw what we didn't want to be, and we wrote songs about that. Craig had more music in him than we knew. We would have an idea, like that a song should be fast. When we heard a key, we'd tell him, *Yeah, that's it, now where should it go?* He would play what popped into his head, and we'd have a song. ■ We did this for six months straight, maybe four or five days a week, a couple hours a day. We got fast, we got tight, we could play our set three times in an hour, and soon we started to write better songs. All we needed was a singer. ■ I knew the perfect guy. He was a bigmouth with a penchant for Bach, martial arts, sci-fi, and the Roman Empire. Plus, he loved Minor Threat, and the Bad Brains made him go berserk. The only trouble was...he didn't really want to be in a band. He had lots of ideas and energy, but getting him to commit to anything that wasn't his idea was *tough.* ■ I managed to get him to a few rehearsals and into the recording studio. I shoved some pieces of paper with words on them in front of him and said, *Okay, try and get this all in in a minute thirty.* He did a good job, and even managed to write a song, but that was about it. He didn't really get into the horror thing, either. I was more into hardcore, but I liked the imagery that horror offered. After all, however, the Misfits still had the ghoul rock thing down pat. Why bother trying to top them, really? ■ We did some shows, and opened for the Misfits once. We did another recording session, and then Bob stopped showing up. One day, not long after that, Glenn asked me if I wanted to start a band with him...

(below) (from left: Bruce and Dom) This is a very important image to me. In front of the house where Rosemary's Babies, Samhain, and even Danzig rehearsed are my best friend and his brother. I went to almost all my shows with Dom. This is my entire adolescence, captured in a single photo.

(above) *Rosemary's Babies in the basement of my parents' house in Lodi. This is where the bands practiced, where the film and photos were developed, and where the T-shirts were printed.*

(above) This was Rosemary's Babies for six month, before we had a singer. We worked very hard to play as fast as we could, and still say what we came to say. That work ethic stayed with me through Samhain and Danzig.

(above) Becki beat me with her riding crop during the show, and the resulting wound being the subject of a song for us. Not a good song, mind you, but a song nonetheless.

(above) We went to see Vice Squad in NYC because Bob had a thing for both U.K. punk and Becki Bondage, Vice Squad's singer. Here he tries to "chat her up," as they say across the pond.

(above) This strip of negatives is from the Vice Squad show, which also featured Bad Brains. That's J.R. in the suspenders going off to Bad Brains, and the fists in the air are Bruce's. He started swinging the moment the band kicked in.

Linguine was a chick who was friends with another girl, Vicki, from Jersey who had a short-lived fanzine called ASSASSIN OF YOUTH. Linguine took these photos and gave them to me. I used her stuff on the Blood Lust 7" EP cover art. I'm grateful to her for giving me the negatives. That was the way things were back then; everyone wanting to help out everyone else in the scene.

ROSEMARY'S BABIES
MAY 15
SUNDAY MATINEE 3:30
GOOD THRASH LIKE IT'S MEANT TO BE.

PHOTO BY THE A.A·N·W·

CBGB's 315 BOWERY

(center) There must have been twenty in CBs that Sunday evening. Little did I know how long the journey would be after I took this first step.

started Samhain as just an extension of what had come before it. Our first show was at the Rock Hotel in New York City. When our guitarist at the time, Lyle Preslar (ex-Minor Threat), saw me with the makeup and Devilock, he said that we could have been the Misfits. But Samhain wasn't the Misfits, at least not to me; it was the next step. ■ I looked at things as if we were carrying on a tradition. That's why I decided to wear a Devilock. Glenn never said he wanted to abandon that look. We still felt connected to the Misfits at the time. For the record, I thought Glenn should have called the band "Glenn Danzig and the somethings." But he wanted a new *band.* He was very into the band concept in those days. I thought the Archangels might be a good band name, or Glenn Danzig and the Archangels. It was to be Samhain though, of course. ■ "Samhain" is the real name for Halloween. The name is Celtic, and was more spiritual then what had gone on in the Misfits. This was about survival, and real-life stuff. Not so much about comic books and late-night horror films, Samhain was more serious. We called our first record *Initium*, Latin for new beginning. That's how we saw Samhain: as a new beginning. ■ Despite all contrary accounts, the band started with Glenn Danzig and Lyle Preslar and Brian Baker from Minor Threat. Glenn went down to D.C. for a few rehearsals. They even recorded a track with Al Pike from Reagan Youth on bass at one point. I love Brian and Lyle, but that configuration never would have worked. ■ When none of those avenues led anywhere, Glenn came to me. He probably knew I could help him get where he wanted to go, and that I wouldn't rock the boat. Good choice. We got together in my basement for the first time and started to work out "All Murder, All Guts, All Fun" and "Black Dream." The next time, I brought in Craig, Rosemary's Babies guitar player, to help flesh out the tunes. It was immediately apparent that I wasn't gonna cut it on drums. This material was a lot harder than either the Misfits songs

or the hyperspeed I was used to in Rosemary's Babies. ■ Soon after, Glenn suggested that I play bass, and that we get Steve from Mourning Noise to play drums. That lineup would be enough for us to start recording. We could have guitar players come in later to beef up the tracks where necessary. He said, *With your personality, you should be out front. Besides, anyone can play bass.* That was good enough for me. I went to Sam Ash on Route 4 in Paramus, New Jersey, and bought the second bass I picked up. First I chose the same bass that James Jamerson had used for all those Motown classics, the Fender Precision. I didn't like it. The neck felt funny—too thick—in my hands. How about the jazz bass? That one felt right, and it came with a hard-shell case, something I would need on the road. Sold. ■ I learned my first song on bass in Steve's bedroom, at his apt in Lodi. We were going to revisit the Misfits' "Horror Business" with a slightly different arrangement. Our version would be "Horror Biz"; that became the start of Samhain. ■ At the Rock Hotel on the night of the band's first show, Glenn was sick. We only had ten songs, and that included a few Misfits tunes. About a thousand people showed up to see the new "supergroup" born from the ashes of the Misfits and Minor Threat. Talk about a trial by fire, for sure. I hadn't played in front of more than a few hundred people in my life, even when opening for the Misfits. I don't remember being nervous, I always had confidence. I felt like I belonged on that stage. ■ The show was a big success, even with Glenn being under the weather. There was only one problem; Lyle was a great guitar player and a terrific guy—but spooky? Spooky, he was not. I guess Glenn didn't even tell him to wear black, because Lyle showed from D.C. wearing jeans and a Minor Threat sweatshirt. We would have to find someone else, someone local. We needed someone who could put up with me and Glenn. Hmmm...

1 ALL HELL BREAKS
2 SAMHAIN
3 BLACK DREAM
4. THE SHIFT
5. THE HOWL
6. DIE, DIE, DIE
7. UNHOLY PASSION
8 ALL MURDER
9. I AM MISERY
10. HALLOWEEN II
11. THE HUNGRY END
12 HORROR BIZ
13. HE WHO CANNOT BE NAMED

FROM THE ASHES OF THE MISFITS & MINOR THREAT....

SAMHAIN

Hell Bent

ROCK HOTEL
113 JANE ST.
at w.side hwy.
279-1995

Adm. $7
doors
open
9pm

SAT. MAR. 31

SEC.   ROW   SEAT
GENERAL ADMISSION
ADVANCE $6.00
AT DOOR $8.00
Ticket#   125
      SAMHAIN

JILJIL PRODUCTIONS PRESENT
      SAMHAIN
SUN MAR 2 1986
         R.P.M.
132 QUEEN'S QUAY EAST
   (FOOT OF JARVIS)
    - ALL AGES -

SEC.   ROW   SEAT
132 QUEEN'S QUAY EAS

NO EXCHANGE OR REF
DOOR OPEN 7:

GENERAL ADMISSI
ADVANCE $
Ticket#

GENERAL ADMISSION
AT DOOR $8.
      SAMHAIN

chapter 2

All Murder, All Guts.

1983-'87

(right) Live photograph by
Jaye S. Clarke, somewhere
on tour in 1985. The Star
Trek shirt pictured is the
very one I'm wearing in
the photo.

Samhain Spring 1984

I took these shots in Glenn's apartment at a point before Damien joined the band and before the *Initium* "blood" cover photos were taken. We needed the band's first-ever promo shots, so we got to work on a setup. I took photos during this period as a form of practice for my craft, and to help develop my look and style. The statues and gargoyles were directly out of Glenn's personal collection. ■ We wound up doing the *Initium* shoot not long after this, and so used a B&W image from that shoot for our first 8x10 promo photo. These are ultra-rare images of the band in one of its earliest lineups, seen here as a mini-set for the first time ever.

(left) Glenn took this one of me out front of Graceland.

(overleaf) This is the shot I really wanted that day; Glenn paying his respects at the King's grave site.

We arranged our first trip to Graceland, around a show in Memphis on September 25, 1984 at the Antenna Club. Glenn likes Elvis a lot but I was the biggest Elvis fan in the band. I couldn't wait to see the house and stroll the grounds; this visit was like going to Church for me. Since many of Glenn's friends and fans call him the "Evil Elvis," I had to take pictures of him there. I think he may have liked the comparisons to Elvis and I think he has great admiration for the man as a singer. Glenn hadn't been to Graceland before, either, so I know he was into being there nearly as much as I was. ■ At the time you couldn't access a lot of the house, and they had yet to establish either the car museum or the racquetball building. Glenn didn't want to make a big deal about getting pictures, so I only shot a few.; kind of a hit-and-run mission, if you will. Here are some highlights of the day.

(left) Glenn with Elvis' mother's pink 1955 Cadillac; the one he bought for her at the beginning of his rise to fame. She never drove it, not even once, and it still sits there today as a loving tribute to her.

We recorded the songs that would be the second Samhain release, *Unholy Passion*, and next we needed some photos of the band for the cover. Getting Glenn to sit down for photos back then was not easy. He decided he would shoot his picture at home, at his leisure. My job was to get the other guys together at my house for studio-type portraits that would work for Glenn's design concept. I got Steve and Damien to show up, and I shot some serious high-contrast stuff that could easily be dropped into any paste-up situation Glenn might have in mind. I combed my hair back for a slightly different look. ■ I was never crazy about the shots, or about the cover, for that matter. Glenn had done a small drawing, which he said was meant to be used for the Misfits' "Devil's Whorehouse," but he'd never got around to using. The image featured a succubus chick with big boobs, wings, and a fur bikini. The song "Unholy Passion" was Glenn's first foray into writing songs about sex and seduction, and he wanted to illustrate the point with a sexy cover. Whatever. ■ The five-song *Unholy Passion* EP turned out to be a bit of a departure from our first release; it was more underground and more tribal. We had taken a step back further into the darkness.

(below) One of the few "band" shots I took for Unholy Passion. *As you can see, I barely had enough time to get into the shot after setting the camera's timer.*

(facing page) This shot is an unseen outtake. I'm wearing one of the eyeball rings I found at C'est Magnifique, a tiny shop in the Village where I used to buy all my rings. I wound up losing the first one on tour somewhere.

THRASHER

Creeping up from the deep dark depths of the catacombs below, the "Unholy Passion" stalks its prey through the mystic crooning of **Sam Hain**. On their second release, **Sam Hain** continue the haunt packed terror with frightfully fearsome harmonies, lunging for the throats with Glenn Danzig's eerie oooing voices commanding the show. Drilling guitar sounds with a drum murmur constantly beating adds to the effect of horror; spookfully achieved. Five ghoulish numbers on this twelve inch, "Moribund," "The Hungry End," "Unholy Passion," "I Am Misery" and a reworked version of **The Misfits** classic "All Hell Breaks Loose." Bring open the gates as the demons celebrate this pagan festival of the dead, **Sam Hain's** "Unholy Passion," a wicked treat for your ear-drums on Plan 9 Records.

(below) Damien took a while to get his look together. He had a hair issue; we used to give him grief about having a white man's afro. Somehow, I captured the complex personality beneath the beer drinking and girl chasing that were his main interests besides Johnny Thunders-style guitar.

(above) Steve Zing showing off his new leather jacket. Glenn and I used to pick on Steve something awful. Steve told me it was one of the reasons he eventually left the band. What can I say? We weren't nice people back then—not like the Prince Charming I am now.

All the ones of Damien and Steve all the ones of ME, I don't know, Ste The ones I checked off are the ones

long developing times, or more expo the features in —

The original Unholy Passion contact sheet, front and back. We would see the photos and select some of our favorites. Then, in this specific case, I wrote notes on the back and handed them over to Glenn for him to see.

(left) After I set everything up just right, I had Glenn snap this one of me.

June 1985

I stole the concept for this lighting from the third *Star Trek* movie. The Klingons had kool lighting. This was also shot in my basement, on a timer, right after Steve Zing left the band. I asked Glenn to comb his hair back so we could get a good look at his face for a change. I think it showed he could still look kool without that wall of hair. ■ I only got four or five shots because someone had a headache or wasn't into it, I can't quite recall. The pictures from this session were never used and remain unseen.

August 1985

For the *November Coming Fire* album shoot, Damien took us up to a local hilltop—a place where he spent his free time throwing empty beer cans into the valley below and dreaming of playing guitar for Iggy Pop. We made a fire and waited for sundown. The sky turned a beautiful purple, the fire threw sparks and smoke into the air, and we posed for the pictures that would grace the back cover of our third record—my personal favorite. ▪ Glenn stood away from the fire during a break. I had Damien pound a burning log into the ground to create the plume of smoke that creeps into the frame of this unused, alternate shot.

Samhain 1986

(left) This limestone angel, a souvenir from one of my many midnight strolls through a favorite graveyard, is still in my collection. The purple and black drape is funeral bunting.

(above, right) I took this shot of the July 1986 Thrasher magazine cover to use as the source image for the first-ever Danzig shirt.

(right) *I completed this drawing shortly before Cliff died. It was made into a T-shirt at one point. We were good friends with Metallica by 1986, and hung out whenever they came to town.*

ALCOHOLLICA

BOSTON ROCK
fashion • style • entertainment

NDIE 49

TM	LM	MOC	ARTIST, TITLE, LABEL, FORMAT
1	1	6	Golden Palominos, *Visions of Excess,* Celluloid, LP/Cass
2	☆	1	Black Flag, *Who's Got the 10½?,* SST, LP/Cass
3	☆	1	Camper Van Beethoven, *II & III,* Pitch a Tent/Rough Trade, LP
4	6	3	Cocteau Twins, *The Pink Opaque,* Relativity, LP/Cass
5	18	8	Dead Milkmen, *Big Lizard in My Backyard,* Fever/Enigma, LP
6	9	2	G.B.H., *Midnight Madness and Beyond,* Combat Core, LP/Cass
7	5	2	Samhain, *November Coming Fire,* Plan 9, LP
8	8	6	Hoodoo Gurus, *Mars Needs Guitars,* Big Time, LP/Cass
9	7	5	Dead Kennedys, *Frankenchrist,* Alternative Tentacles, LP
10	8	4	Collins, Copeland, & Cray, *Showdown,* Alligator, LP/Cass

(above) *On Transylvania Ave. in Columbus, Ohio, with the first great love of my life, Heidi Santelli. I met her during the first Samhain tour, at the Jockey Club in Newport, Kentucky. We were together from 1984 until 1986. When I later moved to L.A., she picked me and John Christ up from the airport. She's a movie producer now.*

(left) *The* BOSTON ROCK *independent record chart. We were in good company.*

HANG ON TO YOUR WORLD, IT'S....

SAMHAIN

LAST RITES PRESENTS

SUN. NOV. 3

SPECIAL GUESTS
MINUTEMEN

PLAN9

Plus
Product 19
&
The Not

cabaret
METRO

3730 N. Clark, Chicago, Illinois 60613
ALL-AGES   549-0203   6:00pm

1985
The Chicago Bloodbath

Ever since pouring blood over our heads for the cover of *Initium*, we talked about recreating that look onstage in a live setting. Somewhere along the way to the Metro in Chicago, Glenn decided he wanted to do it there. We looked at the blood idea as both a way to create a Samhain "spectacular," and to celebrate the last show of the tour. ▪ We originally wanted to rig the scene like CARRIE, with buckets of blood in the rafters that would dump all over us, but there wasn't a way we could set that up with The Metro's stage ceiling being so high. Anyway, we had left the buckets back in New Jersey! ▪ We tried to figure out how to get actual pig blood for the occasion. After all, this was Chicago, where they were known to butcher stuff from time to time! It should have been a breeze, right? Not really. And the people who ran the Metro were not into this idea one bit—no way, no how. ▪ Instead, we ran to a local grocery store and collected the ingredients for the next best thing: Hollywood blood! Glenn knew the recipe, and we set out to make a massive batch for our stage show. We bought four bottles of Karo Syrup and a load of red food coloring, and then heading back to the Metro. We were set. ▪ We decided to just dump the mix on one another, but we only ended up using three of four bottles. Our drummer London May didn't want it dumped on his head. We left a pool of blood at least eight feet wide on the dressing room floor. It looked like a murder scene; it was awesome! ▪ The reaction from the crowd was amazing, as no one had ever done that before. We ended up playing the whole show covered in sticky Hollywood blood, and left one hell of a mess for someone to clean up. Simply put, we had a great night.

(below) Here's one of the four bottles of blood from that day in Chicago. It still has my name on top, and sits among the skulls and dust in my vast collection.

(facing page and previous overleaf) These pics from the Metro show were sent to me a few weeks later by the photographer; a big fan named Ted Domurat. He captured the sights and mood in all their blood-covered glory. Many thanks to Ted for not only being there, but for sharing these photos all these years later.

The Ritz
07/14/86

The Ritz in New York City was a big gig for any band during those years. The Misfits had played there in 1981. I had seen many shows there: everyone from Motörhead to Joan Jett, and from Dwight Yoakam to Gary Numan. The Ritz was a great gig in NYC, and headlining there was a big deal. We always drew a big crowd there, and I loved that place. ■ For our second show at the Ritz, we had to do something special. We had to attract even more attention. Damien and I decided to dress formal, so we dug through the thrift stores and found tuxedos with tails and the works. I scored a horribly ruffled shirt, and he managed to acquire a plain purple one. Mine was better. ■ Glenn wanted to do the "blood encore." That worked for me just fine—by then the tux would be history, anyway! Since we all came from punk rock backgrounds, we were used to theatricality. This was show business, after all. At this point, only the metal bands were doing anything special on stage. This was our way of showing that maybe we could make the move to the big leagues. I know Glenn had some misgivings about trying to make the jump. After all, as he told me, there was no going back if we failed. ■ A New York show always brought out the best in the band. Our first-ever gig was in New York. Now one of our most important shows had us mowing through the "hits," like "Black Dream," "Mother of Mercy," "Unholy Passion," "In My Grip," and a host of others. Samhain was awash

in intensity, sweat, and mayhem; in other words, a typical night in New York. ■ At the time, I didn't know Rick Rubin was in the audience. I didn't know this night would be a major turning point. Who knew this lineup would never play together in public again? Who could have known that this was the beginning of the end for Samhain? ■ By now, we had three albums out, plenty of songs to choose from, so we played our usual twelve-to-thirteen-song set. Glenn was in a good mood, so we treated the crowd to a couple of Misfits songs. You know, just in case the evening wasn't memorable enough already! After the set, we were totally spent. We said goodnight and disappeared up the spiral staircase to the dressing room. We only took a moment to catch our breath, poured the blood on each other, and descended the stairs once again. ■ It's difficult to blow people's minds in New York. We didn't have that problem. Like the Chicago Bloodbath before the previous November, no one had done this. It made us even crazier. We took the stage again, and the fans loved it. They smeared the blood all over Glenn's chest, and wiped it on their faces like we were all involved in a Pagan ritual sacrifice. And we were, I suppose. Something was dying that night, but we were also giving life to something new; we just didn't know it at that moment. Maybe Rubin did. He met us in the dressing room and described the event using his favorite word, *incredible.* I remember him handing me a business card. The rest is a blur. We were well on our way to another place altogether. I don't think Glenn ever doubted that this thing could be *big.* Of course, as it played out in the years to come, he was right.

(facing page, top) This is right before the Ritz show. I was trying on my newly-acquired fancy duds. Photo by Mom.

(The Ritz) All live photography by Kon Akiyama

89

Ron Akiyama
photographer

The amazing photos displayed here were taken by Ron Akiyama. Images like his and Ted Domurat's from Chicago allow this book the perspective of the fan, even if for just a little while. I met Ron in New Jersey at the Elmwood Park Indoor Flea Market, a frequent haunt of Bruce, Dom, J.R. and myself on weekends. Ron sat in a booth selling his photos, mostly rejects that weren't chosen for publication. He had great stuff, all the big names of the day. I first noticed his shots of Joan Jett. I was a fan of hers, and struck up a conversation with him. I knew I had seen him shooting her at shows. I wanted to know how he knew her, and if he was for hire. ▪ I told him I was in a band that could use some quality live shots. We had a Ritz show coming up where we were gonna do the Bloodbath for the encore. He said it was something like $300 to $400 to shoot the whole show in both B&W and color. *What a bargain*, I thought—as I think you'll agree. Ron and I became friends, and he wound up shooting the first-ever photos of Danzig a few years later.

(left) Those are Kirk Hammett's and James Hetfield's autographs on Damien's guitar. We had a day off after a Bloomington, Indiana, show and we heard Metallica were opening for Ozzy Osbourne at Market Square Arena in Indianapolis. We drove up to see the show and hang out. Those guys asked us for our autographs before Damien could ask for theirs. I never got any signatures, actually, but Hetfield did sleep on my couch once.

Out With The Old, '86

Once Rick Rubin came into the picture, things started to change. He went right to work on Glenn. They hung out together, went to wrestling matches, went out to dinner, and talked a lot about music and performers. ■ Rick got more interested in singers like Roy Orbison, and we got more interested in rap music, his stock in trade. Glenn and Rick were big influences on each other, and together they crafted a master plan for world domination. ■ Rick didn't have much use for the band, he was mainly interested in Glenn. One by one, guys were dropped. Damien was the first to go. Glenn wasn't a big one for confrontations then, so when he told Damien down in my basement in Lodi that he was out of the band, Glenn did so without any joy or malice. I could see it wasn't easy for him, but we felt that we needed to change in order to move forward. Damien never asked why or pleaded his case, he just packed up his gear and left. I haven't seen him since, though I heard he later played with Iggy Pop. He was, and probably still is, a really nice guy. ■ Now we needed a guitar player. We tried out a lot of people on our own at first, but ultimately we set up auditions in NYC at Aerosmith's Top Cat rehearsal studio. Lots of players came and went, including longtime Ramones producer Daniel Rey, and Billy Hilfiger—brother of the famous designer. I played all the auditions in full makeup, just so newcomers knew what they were in for. One day, Rubin pulled me aside and asked if didn't I think that this whole Devilock thing would alienate a large part of our potential audience? Didn't I want as many people as possible to hear our music? Wasn't that what was most important? Just something to think about. That

120 West 28th Street
New York, N.Y. 10001
(212) 807-9494

TOP CAT
S O U N D   S T U D I O S ,   I N C.

did make sense, and, truthfully, as I got older I was starting to feel a little less comfortable in makeup and a Devilock. I would always feel like a monster, but wasn't sure I wanted to make it so obvious anymore. Looking back now, I'm sure Rick figured I would be gone soon enough, anyway—but I wasn't in fear of losing my spot on bass. After all, Glenn and I formed this band, and it was still him and me against the world. ■ London May was not cutting it on drums, that became obvious during the auditions. Things were moving fast, and you had to move with the times or get left behind. He did provide us with one thing before I told him he was out of the band: John Christ. London's father worked with John's father, or something like that, and London's dad happened to mention his son's band was looking for a new guitar player. John, who was into Judas Priest, Iron Maiden, and Ted Nugent, drove up from Baltimore in a tiny car to audition for some punk rock guy and a rap producer he had never heard of. Who were these guys? We made him wait out in the lobby for hours while we tried out a few other players. He was the last guitarist of the evening. He had learned the required three songs, but he was pretty pissed when he walked in. He threw down his cord and set up his gear. ■ This guy was different. We could tell right away. He knew his stuff, and he handled our songs with ease. We all sat down and watched him solo, and we were blown away. We weren't used to this. We didn't know any metal guys, except for Kirk and James from Metallica, so this was a new world to us. Rubin loved him, and so did London and I, but Glenn wasn't so sure. This was not a punk rock guy; he was the polar opposite, and that may have rubbed Glenn the wrong way. ■ Rick assured him that this was the guy. He said, *Let me talk to him. I'll take him to dinner, and I'll tell him what the deal is.* There were more auditions. During that time, John kept calling Glenn's answering machine, and leaving three minutes of down-strumming guitar as a message. He wanted the

In With The New. '87

gig, and he was trying to prove he could handle it. That made an impression, and Glenn relented. John was now in Samhain. ■ The axe was about to fall again, and this time London May had his head on the block. Glenn asked me to give him the bad news. For the record, he was totally shocked. It wasn't easy for me to do. London was a nice guy and a pretty good drummer, but Glenn already had to play on half of our last record. Now London wasn't getting the new songs at all. Anyone who knows will tell you, the drummer is the whole band. We had to let him go. ■ For the next album, titled *Samhain Grim*, we had recorded four or five tracks with London on drums and Glenn on guitar. When John joined the band, we wasted no time having him lay down guitar on the new songs. He also overdubbed Damien's parts on "Halloween II," which shouldn't have been done, but Glenn figured if you weren't on the record you didn't have to be paid for it. ■ We had "Possession," "Twist a Cain" (as it was called then), "Lords of the Left Hand," "The Birthing," and a Leiber and Stoller song written for Elvis called "Trouble." Of course, now we needed a drummer. Two names came up: "Philthy Animal" Phil Taylor, the original Motörhead stick master; and Chuck Biscuits, the punk rock Keith Moon. Glenn had become enamored with the double-kick drum sound used by all the metal bands. I think that's why he liked the idea of Phil. I had only seen Chuck play with the Circle Jerks on a TV show called ROCK PALACE. He was, as Rubin liked to say, *Incredible.* ■ Glenn was at Rick's apartment in the city, and they got Chuck on the phone. Supposedly Rubin said: *This is Rick Rubin and I'm sitting here with Glenn Danzig. He's putting together a new band. What would it take to get you to join?* Chuck replied, *A plane ticket.* And that was that. We now had a great guitar

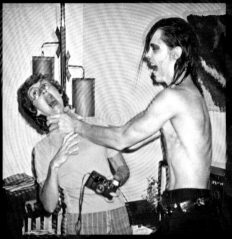

(left) Goofing around with my mom, as photographed by my dad.

player, an amazing drummer, one of the best singer-songwriters of his generation, and a mediocre bass player. Oh well, I would get better. ■ There was no audition for Chuck, he just showed up with a kick pedal and a pack of smokes, and went to work. I'll never know how I held onto my job at this point. Rick didn't want me there, but thankfully Glenn did. Maybe it was because he could trust me. I was loyal, and he wasn't ready to give up that link to the past. Maybe it was because I made him laugh, I'm not quite sure. ■ With all the pieces in place, we started rehearsing. The two new guys were great, and we clicked right away. We settled into a rehearsal space in Saddle Brook, New Jersey, where we would soon meet our future sound man. We worked on the songs three days a week, three hours a day. John and I went to the gym five or six days a week, as well. Occasionally, Rubin would come to rehearsals, or we would go back to Top Cat where the new songs were painstakingly arranged and perfected. ■ At a restaurant called Exterminator Chili in NYC, Glenn and Rick brought up the next order of business. We're gonna call the band "Danzig." To which I replied, *Just like Bon Jovi.* The new band needed a new name, and so the band Danzig was born. Rick had succeeded in getting what he wanted: a hand-picked super group with two punk rock icons; a bar-band headbanger who could blow your mind; and a bass player who looked good in pictures! Now we had to get our new songs down on wax. ■ First we recorded a song for the movie LESS THAN ZERO, for which Rick was music director. The song was nicked from the theme of the '60s film, TO SIR, WITH LOVE. After a few passes I didn't want to play on it anymore, so, instead, the song was credited to Glenn Danzig and the Power and Fury Orchestra.

(right) Hanging out with my dad. Photograph taken by my mom.

95

Danzig: Death American: *One of the earliest Fiend Art Paintings.*

chapter 3
1987-1995
At the Top
of the World

Sorcerer Sound at 19 Mercer Street in New York was where we started tracking the first Danzig album. We recorded all the basic tracks there, then scrapped them all except for "Mother" (*I think*), and wound up starting over at the Record Plant. Overdubs, overdubs overdubs. Rubin had me going over the bass for "Am I Demon" until I could do it in my sleep. I don't believe in perfection when it comes to recording. I go for the feel. Mistakes are okay if the groove is there, and this band was about that bump-and-grind kind of groove. I hated it. ■ Two of the songs from the final Samhain session made it to the new record: "Twist a Cain" (now "Twist of Cain") and "Possession." Just for kicks, James from Metallica came in to sing backups on both tracks. We also recorded "Trouble" again, which didn't make it onto the album. ■ I had never worked so hard on a record. Neither had Biscuits, who had to run into the control room after every take while Rubin told him to hit the hi-hat here, put two kicks there; boom-tat, boom-tat. Poor Chuck, you could see him looking up in the air, trying to remember *bop-um-do-bow*, and all the rest of it. What a nightmare. ■ Rick liked AC/DC, Black Sabbath, and Led Zeppelin. He had two styles of production, either AC/DC or Sabbath/Zeppelin. He would strip away all the bullshit, and bring it down to the bare bones; starting with the drums. He thought Phil Rudd of AC/DC was God. Just like he had done with the Cult on their *Electric* album only months before, he made the production very sparse and the sound very dry. Good thing he liked the driving eighth-note stuff on bass, because that was about all I could do at the time. In the end, the record was well-received, for many of those reasons. I thought the songs were great, but that the album sounded awful. John Christ hated it. Meanwhile, Rick had been talking about splitting up his record company Def Jam, and moving the business to California. One fine day, Glenn said, *I'm moving to L.A. What are you guys gonna do?*

(right) This was day one for the first album, and I wanted to capture the moment. (left to right) Glenn Danzig (he shared an interest in porn with Rick Rubin); John Christ; George Drakoulias (Rick's whipping boy at the time, now a successful producer himself); Dave Bianco (engineer); Rick Rubin; yours truly; and Chuck Biscuits. I put the camera on a timer and got us all to sit still. Hard to believe this was over twenty-five years ago.

Sorcerer Sound
NYC '87

Sorcerer Sound
24 AND 48 TRACK
AUTOMATED RECORDING
19 MERCER ST. NEW YORK, NY (212) 226-0480

(facing page) *This is one of the only photos I ever took of Glenn Danzig in the vocal booth. He let me shoot him however I wanted. The sign was mine, of course.*

(above) *The three cogs in the big Danzig machine. I'm holding my Aria Pro II bass, my backup from Samhain. John's wearing a skull shirt I printed for him.*

(below) *This could have been one of the reasons the sessions ended. We couldn't find another pedal that would work for Chuck. By the time we located a replacement, we likely had moved to another studio.*

(above) *John with the true love of his life, his B.C. Rich Bich. We hadn't yet corrupted him.*

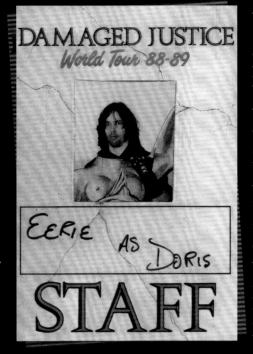

DAMAGED JUSTICE
World Tour 88-89

EERIE AS DORIS

STAFF

We first met Metallica in San Francisco in 1985. The whole band came to see Samhain at the Mabuhay Gardens on Broadway. Cliff Burton turned Kirk Hammett and James Hetfield onto the Misfits, and, over time, we became friends. We saw each other when we could. When they were going on tour in Europe to promote *...And Justice for All*, we all thought it would be fun to tour together. ■ They asked us to do three weeks. I don't remember if we had to pay a "buy-on" to get the gig, but we probably did. Oh God, Europe. Chuck, Glenn, and I wanted no part of it, and that's why we called it the "3 Weeks in Hell Tour." ■ Metallica wasn't as big then as they would become in a few years, so we didn't play arenas, but mostly large theaters and clubs. The gigs were still small enough for us all to hang out, get drunk, and look for trouble. So we did just that. ■ I wasn't used to the iceless Jack & Cokes, warm beer, mystery meats, and room temperature cheeses provided by the U.K. venues. Metallica did have a catering crew traveling with the tour, so we got at least one hot meal a day. Our mode of transportation was a passenger van, and the long distances from show to show were a bit much. If we wanted to something to eat or drink, there were no 7-11s anywhere to be found. We quickly learned to carry candy on us in order to survive. ■ I don't think our album was out just yet. We did about eight or nine songs a night, and nobody really knew what to make of us. We surely weren't metal enough. The Misfits Legend had not grown into what it is today. Only die-hard fans knew who Glenn was. Opening for Metallica—or Slayer, like we did later—was no easy task. Playing to a hostile crowd—some

were still into spitting, by the way—was great. *You hate us? Well, we hate you right back!* Ours was more of a gang mentality. Fuck you if you don't like it. We had a few occasions where we were asked for encores, but, knowing the protocol, we didn't take them or try to show up the headliners. ■ It was great to hang out with other musicians I liked. You see how things are going for your friends at a certain level, and you learn from their experiences. We could see what it would be like for us if, and, or when we got there. People followed us all around. They watched us eat fish and chips, and took photos. Fun? Yeah, but not out of control. There were border crossings, ferry trips, blood pudding, eggs with orange yolks, and a different beer in every town. I almost never got Jack Daniel's and had to make do with Glenfiddich, or some other intoxicant. James and I had fans believing we were brothers who were separated after our parents divorced! Soon, the consensus in the business was that we would be the next Metallica; that's what was expected from us. So putting us together on tour and talking to their management company seemed like a natural progression. ■ We were learning how to be a real working band on the road, and, for once, we put priorities in their proper order. Naturally, we also stayed up late drinking, talking, and seeing what we could get away with! I think Metallica's management looked upon us as a bad influence. I take the blame for most of that. Yeah, we were definitely an influence, but not a bad one entirely. We must have made an impression; after those three weeks, we wouldn't get another Metallica tour for six years!

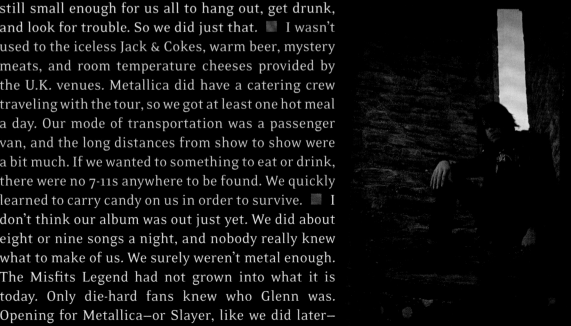

SHOW TIMES

DOORS   6.30

DANZIG   7.30

       8.15

INTERVAL

METALLICA   8.45

CLOSE   10.45

(left) As you can see, the Doors opened the show.

(right) This is the look Chuck would give you that meant, "Are you kidding me?"

(left) John in leather, playing one of his Les Pauls. Rick and Glenn liked that guitar, so he tried a few, but I think he's more of a Fender guy.

(left) Jason Newsted was an Elvis fan, so we had that in common. Although he was kind of guarded and hard to read, he was a very dedicated, determined, and intense guy. I gave him his first pair of wristbands. That's the Doris statue in the background, looking on.

(top left) The Hamster walking into our dressing room...in the middle of their set! This must have been during the drum solo. I can't believe I had the camera in my hand at that moment.

(bottom left) James Hetfield and Glenn toasting the pairing of our two bands. James is wearing our U.K. tour shirt.

Her Black Wings
the Videoshoot

Our boy Vinnie Giordano shot this one of the band with Becky Mullen. God Don't Like It.

(above) Glenn with his Super 8 camera, shooting me while I shot him. That's John in the makeup chair.

(right) Glenn took this one of me with the "scary sky." I shaved for this video, and I've regretted it ever since. Not a good look for me.

(Upper left) Glenn and director
of photography Vinnie Giordano,
checking out her black
wings. Becky came from the
women's wrestling league, G.L.O.W.,
where she was known as "Sally the
Farmer's Daughter."

(Upper right) This was Glenn's
first real shot at directing one
of our music videos.

(Front) Glenn was in the best
shape I had ever seen him.

DANZIG

GOD DON'T LIKE IT
SUMMER '89
GUEST

(above) Chuck's brother, Dimwit (also a drummer), visits us on tour. The world lost a good man in '94 when Dimwit left us far too soon.

(above) I set this shot up and gave the camera to my L.A. girlfriend Renee Morris. I was a James Dean fan, and I wanted to visit Griffith Observatory, where they filmed REBEL WITHOUT A CAUSE.

On the Road: 1989

After our move to Los Angeles, with our first record in the stores and a few bad videos under our belts, we spent most of our time touring. The Metallica "3 Weeks in Hell" U.K. tour gave way to the "Not of This World" and "God Don't Like It" tours, where a lot of these photos were taken. We sold out Jezebel's in Anaheim, the Palace in Hollywood, and then we did a live KNAC broadcast. In the middle of all of this, we traveled to San Francisco on January 5 to play at the Stone, a small club across the street from the one Samhain had played. It was a step up, mind you, but not a prestige gig by any means. Kirk Hammett and James Hetfield came down, and of course that made the show a happening. They got up and did two songs with us for the encore—I think "Halloween II" and "London Dungeon." We also filmed stuff for inclusion on our upcoming home video release. MTV wasn't playing any of the videos we made, so we figured we would give our fans something for home, so they could watch the clips to their heart's content. That first home video was eventually certified gold. ■ Once, when we were touring through the South, the whole band went to see Elvis. This was my third time, I think, and the guys got a kick out of taking the private tour of the house (reserved for visiting rock stars). We drove right up the driveway, and we could hang out as long as we wanted. Every time a tour guide told us a story, the guys would look at me to see if they had gotten it right. Sometimes they did, sometimes they didn't. Our tour manager Andrew was there, and I had him take some shots of the band. ■ All the while that we were there, Chuck was making fun. Glenn joined in, because they thought I would get mad if they dared not show the King the proper respect. Visiting Graceland is like going to church for me. I didn't want any monkey business. The way they were acting was just like a scene in Spinal Tap. They dared me to hit on one of the more attractive tour guides. *Maybe you could bang her on Elvis' bed!* I bet I could have—that would have been kool. ■ In the meantime, the band kept getting better, playing bigger places, and selling more records. Things were good. We could always put asses in the seats. We often sold out venues that bigger bands couldn't fill. It was great playing all over the country, having a nice bus to travel, and meeting the people who were buying our records. Nice work if you can get it; if you ever get the chance, I recommend that you try.

(this page) This is another Jaye Clarke pic from a date on our Southern tour of 1989. What was it that James said every night? Oh yeah, "Cheers everybody!"

DANZIG

ACCESS ALL AREAS

(right) I told Andrew, our tour manager, what I wanted in this shot and he almost got it! Chuck is wearing the big Elvis belt I made for him.

ADMIT ONE
NO REFUNDS
DO NOT DETACH

"Elvis Up Close"
Museum
Graceland
MEMPHIS, TENNESSEE

"Elvis Up Close"

188956

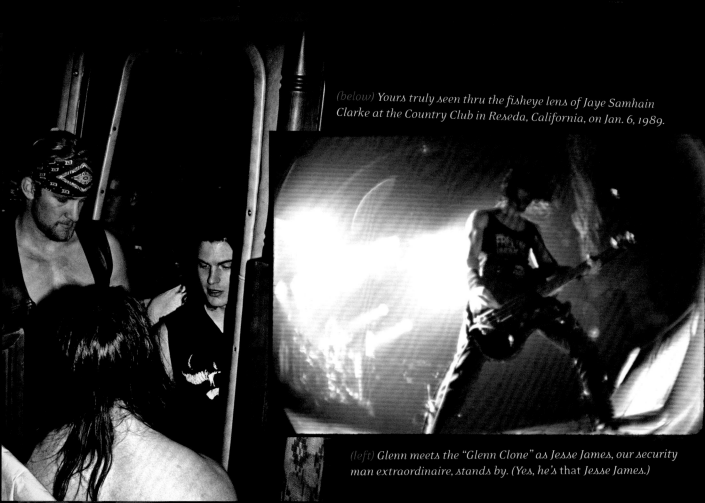

(below) Yours truly seen thru the fisheye lens of Jaye Samhain Clarke at the Country Club in Reseda, California, on Jan. 6, 1989.

(left) Glenn meets the "Glenn Clone" as Jesse James, our security man extraordinaire, stands by. (Yes, he's that Jesse James.)

(below) *This is after a Metallica gig somewhere. I must have seen them fifty times on that tour.*

(right) *On our bus with Pushead, the artist who had done the Misfits Evil Eye T-shirt back in the day; yet another connection between Glenn and Metallica. At one point, practically every shirt Metallica used a Pushead design.*

(left) *This is outside the Stone in San Francisco on Jan. 5, 1989. James looks like the Cowardly Lion, doesn't he? That's our bus driver and my good buddy, Randy Calloway, in the background.*

Blood & Tours
1990

(right) Jesse James in Amsterdam, outside the American Hotel. After he left us, Jesse got rich and famous from his West Coast Choppers business, along with his TV show MONSTER GARAGE.

(above) Glenn started making Samhain shirts, so me and Jaye Clarke had to try them out. Jaye is a fine photographer, outsider artist, and close friend for over twenty years.

(left) One of my favorite subjects, Chuck, at Disneyland.

(below) Glenn Danzig out sightseeing in Koln, Germany.

(top right) In bed with two Cycle Sluts From Hell. My good friend Vas Kallas (now in Hanzel und Gretyl), Queen Vixen, and her sister Lisa help me relax after the Beacon Theatre show in NYC.

(above) The lovely Renee Morris on our bus with my good friend and Danzig soundman and keyboard player, Rick Dittamo.

1. LONG WAY BACK FROM HELL
2. SNAKES OF CHRIST
3. ~~AM I DEMON~~ AM I DEMON
4. MOTHER
5. DEVILS PLAYTHING
6. TIRED OF BEING ALIVE
7. ~~SHE RIDES~~ SHE RIDES
8. 777
9. ~~BLOOD + TEARS~~ BLOOD + TEARS
10. PAIN IN THE WORLD
11. ↑   ↑
12. TWIST OF CAIN
13. HER BLACK WINGS
14. GIRL
15. HUNTER
16. EVIL THING
    NOT OF THIS WORLD

*(above) Fall 1990
headlining tour set list,
written by Glenn*

TONIGHT'S PERFORMANCE

DOORS OPEN **9:00**   SHOWTIME _____

OPEN MEAL _____

C.O.C. FROM **9:30** TO **10:00**

SET CHANGE   SoundGarden FROM **10:15** **11:25**

SET CHANGE   DANZIG FROM **12** **1:15**

PROMOTER Rep. DOUG SUTLER

STAGE MANAGER _____

THANK YOU

*(above) Chris Cornell of
Soundgarden at the Celebrity
Theatre in Phoenix on 8/31/90*

*(lower left) See how well we treated our
opening acts? Chuck, his brother Bob, and
Rick decided to give Warrior Soul a little grief
on the Lucifuge tour. That's a whole case of
duct tape holding their van together.*

A SPECIAL EARLY EVENING CONCERT
DANZIG and SOUNDGARDEN
WITH SPECIAL GUESTS C.O.C.
(CORROSION OF CONFORMITY)

FIRST AVENUE   701 FIRST AVE. NO.
MINNEAPOLIS, MN

SUNDAY • AUG. 5, 1990
DOORS OPEN 4:00 PM • SHOWTIME 5:00 PM
ALL AGE CONCERT

DANZIG
WITH
SOUNDGARDEN

AND
CORROSION OF CONFORMITY

MONDAY, AUGUST 13TH **7:30PM**
TICKETS AT TICKETMASTER
AND THE RECORD PEDDLER   **CONCERT HALL**

A CPI PRODUCTION

the Record Plant '91

We did not turn into the next Metallica, and so Rick Rubin was always busy and not around much, if at all, for our third album. We did not care. We had handled ourselves before, and we could do it again. We still gave him executive producer credit, of course. After all, he was putting up the cash. The band was at its best. We were super tight, and we could play the new material in our sleep. Glenn said he would produce this one. That was fine with me, as long as he didn't try to mix it! ■ The songs were strong, and we had an engineer we liked. I was excited to get to the Record Plant and start cutting tracks. The Record Plant is a famous studio in L.A. where all the biggest musicians in history had recorded, and now we were there, too. The setting was perfect; the lights were low, the vibe was great, and we moved quickly. Most of the masters were first takes. Sometimes we only did two takes. All told, we did fourteen songs in four days—pretty good for any band. We were really on a roll. For me, running into Prince in the lounge made this session even more special. ■ With an extra day left over to track after all our album work was completed, Glenn and I went to Tower Records on Sunset to look for some music. He wanted to cover a T. Rex song. We found a box set with "Buick MacKane." I listened to the song a few times, since I hadn't heard the track before. Chuck and

I worked out what we would play, while John wasn't too sure about his parts. We ended up doing three or four takes, not intending for it to be released, just something for fun. ■ We moved to Studio C for guitar overdubs, leads, and fixing up the rhythm tracks. John always did amazing stuff. This time, to a certain extent, he had more freedom to do what he wanted. He mostly worked alone with the engineer, and came up with what I consider to be some of his greatest work. ■ For the vocals, with no one to push him or make him do take after take, Glenn was back in the driver's seat. He knew what he wanted, what he could and couldn't do. If he was satisfied, that was all that mattered. There is some great singing on *Danzig III*, to say the very least. ■ The mix was done at A&M, the old Charlie Chaplin Studios in Hollywood, where we had done some videos. Everyone-who-was-anyone tracked or mixed there. It was not unusual to see a bunch of *Playboy* girls going to the sound stage, or to hear Steven Tyler doing his thing in the next room. We brought in a mixer. With Glenn supervising, we finished what was, in my opinion, the real essence of the band on record. We had hit our stride. When the record was released, *How the Gods Kill* cracked BILLBOARD's Top 20 and ROLLING STONE gave us four stars. Now all we needed was to see if we could get a giant Danzig skull made in time to go on the next world tour.

(left) Often Glenn would have the ideas stuck in his head and John would help bring them out, usually giving Glenn four or five ways to say what he wanted. Without any doubt, it was a really good system for us.

NO WOMEN OF ANY KIND ON CONSOLE

(above & left) John Christ, in the hat I got him in Tijuana, overdubbing on a Strat with engineer Nick "the Pig" Didia.

(above) Glenn played piano on the Misfits' "Cough/Cool" single, and continued to overdub keyboard parts on all our records.

(above) The band had more to do with this record than the first two. Chuck and John discussing a track as we worked.

(left) I wanted to capture a quiet moment in the studio, and here ended up with one of my all-time favorite shots.

Gods Kill Video '92

Glenn was an artist and a collector, and he was into a bunch of kool shit. He made a deal for us to use artwork from the Swiss artist, HR Giger, for the cover of *Danzig III*. Giger created the *Alien* character, and now he was persuaded to do his own interpretation of the Danzig skull to augment an existing piece he had already done. Very kool, indeed. At the time, he had only done one other significant cover that I knew of, for Emerson, Lake, and Palmer's *Brain Salad Surgery*. ▪ How Glenn met sculptor and special effects man Norman Cabrera, I don't recall, but Norman made us a headpiece for a hot chick to wear on her head. The costume looked exactly like the "The Master and Margarita" painting on our album cover. It was an unbelievable work that included multiple tongues that moved when triggered, and had octopus-like appendages. Norman and I remain friends and he continues to work on big Hollywood films. ▪ We hired a couple of girls, "borrowed" some props on the studio lot, and took over a big Hollywood sound stage.

I loved doing this stuff, and the down time between takes gave me a chance to take pictures. I documented the two-day shoot in lovely B&W. I also have lots of behind-the-scenes video. We did all the band stuff on the first day, from multiple angles. They put us up on high platforms to film us solo, which I wasn't too crazy about! We were finally making a big-budget video. Even though the song wasn't going to be a single, I felt like the band was starting to get some respect from the record company, money-wise. ▪ The next day we did all the insert stuff with the girls and Norman's headpiece. I took a few shots of Norman with his labor of love. When the video was done, we had some time and film left over, so we shot footage for the song, "Bodies." That's why it looks like people are milling about in that video—they really were! The "Bodies" video didn't see the light of day until years later. Even though I still didn't know how or why the gods kill, I thought doing the video was a blast and I felt like a rock star.

(above) One big happy family: The band poses with man-of-the-hour Norman Cabrera and his then-wife, Mimi, on the "How the Gods Kill" set. Without Norman's terrific headpiece, there wouldn't be much of a video.

(opposite page) After cutting his teeth, on the "Her Black Wings" video, Glenn was in charge of this one all the way. Here he directs one of the girls how to look slutty in a Danzig video.

All Access Pass '92

(below) Tour manager
Marc Sokol in Europe

(right) Vas & Manray: "We are from New Country."

(left) The original Sunset Grill in
Hollywood, next to Guitar Center

(left) Der Tanja backstage in Europe

GUEST

(left) Too much headbanging gave me and John Christ bad backs. Here John works out the kinks in his upside-down machine.

(above) DJ, Jim, Morgan, Dittamo, Jesse, and Chuck waiting by our bus

Black Sabbath GUEST

venue ATL 7/26 date SPANK

(above) With Tony Iommi. Fuck yeah!

(above) "I also play keyboards...'cause I can do that, bro."

(above) With Rob Zombie at the HR Giger exhibit. We got a private showing, and I asked HR to sign my Danzig III *album.*

(below) Two dark artists meet and decide what to order from a local Chinese restaurant! (I'm kidding...)

(above) Giger had a great dining room set. Here Rob wonders how he can sneak this chair past customs!

(opposite page) Giger the artist regales us with one of his many tales.

MCP presents

TOWN & COUNTRY

DANZIG

DANZIG

THU.
10th SEP.
7:00pm

In Concert + Special Guests
THURSDAY 10 SEPTEMBER 1992

£7.50
Advance

Doors   7:00pm
Showtime 7:30pm
Advance £7.50

1848

1848

t&c 1   9-17 HIGHGATE ROAD,   PLEASE NOTE
KENTISH TOWN,   THERE IS LIMITED PARKING
LONDON NW5 1JY   IN KENTISH TOWN

(left) Our trip to Scotland included a search for the Aleister Crowley house, one of the highlights of my time with Danzig.

(left) We planned a documentary of the tour. Here Glenn is being filmed at Loch Ness.

(far right) MTV's Dirty Black Summer *special. We pose with Riki Rachtman outside one of Mad King Ludwig's castles in Bavaria. Glenn loved it when I gave Riki a hard time; we both gave him grief during our interview segments.*

(right) There's almost no light inside the throne room at Mad Ludwig's place, but I still managed to get a shot of Glenn admiring the ceiling paintings.

TOUR PERSONNEL

BAND

GLENN DANZIG
CHUCK BISCUITS
EERIE VON
JOHN CHRIST

CREW

NEIL SCHAEFER
RICK DITTAMO
JEFF 'JEBI' KRITZ
GREG 'CRASH' HEARN
STEVE MORGAN
JIM COPPOLA
D.J. WHITE
JESSIE JAMES
DENNIS KEIFFER
DUNCAN HOARE
MARTIN NICHOLAS
RICHARD MCLEOD
STEVE HARE
LES JOHNSON
FERHAN SAKARYA

TOUR RELAT

(left) Mr. Showbiz! It was difficult to get Rob to stand still for a serious photo. He was a fun guy, and we got to be good friends.

0191

SEC   ROW   SEAT

COMPLIMENTARY
NOV 23, 1992

ADMIT ONE THIS DATE ONLY

JAM/Company 7 & First Avenue present

DANZIG
WHITE ZOMBIE
with special guest
and KYUSS

FIRST AVENUE, NO.
7th St. entry

MONDAY • NOVEMBER 23, 1992
DOORS OPEN 7:00 PM • SHOWTIME 8:00 PM

ALL AGE CONCERT
THIS TICKET DOES NOT GUARANTEE ADMISSION WHEN CLUB
HAS REACHED LEGAL CAPACITY.
OUR SUGGESTION IS EARLY ARRIVAL.

701 FIRST AVE. NO.
MINNEAPOLIS, MN

NO REFUND-NO PRICE-NO EXCHANGE

COMP

SEC

CON

CO

danzig
vip
how the gods kill
world tour
1992-1993

(left) Sean Yseult and Rob Zombie in Chicago. I found a good overhead light source, but, of course, Rob wouldn't play it straight.

(above) Downstairs in a St. Louis Dungeon, Rick Dittamo and Rob share a quiet moment reading the paper.

(above) Renee Morris and John relax before a show. Talk about hair care!

(above) White Zombie during sound check

In Moral Servitude
The Thrall Sessions

(right) Chuck Biscuits would often draw in the studio when not recording. Here he relaxes between takes.

(above) John helps Glenn lay down some of that "Samhain" kind of guitar on one of the songs. He's using his favorite Les Paul Junior.

(above) *These two dark artists really are ordering food from Glenn's favorite Thai restaurant, Chan Dara.*

(above) *I set up the camera with a timer and caught the band recording an actual take.*

(both pages) Glenn listens to playback of our version of Elvis' "Trouble." The song was recorded by Samhain and at nearly every Danzig session after that.

On The Road: 1993
Also featuring the photography of Jaye S. Clarke

(below) Besides Metallica and Black Sabbath, we opened five shows for labelmates Slayer. Here Tom Araya visits us before a show and meets Gen from the Genitorturers.

(above) May 23, 1993, Hammerjacks, Baltimore. Photo by Jaye S. Clarke

thrall-demonsweatlive

USA / JAPAN / AUSTRALIA
SUMMER TOUR 1993

(above) The crew, led by Rick Dittamo, races through the airport on our way home.

(above) Chuck wraps his fingers before a show. He killed himself on stage, night after night, and was both an incredibly hard worker and a great showman.

(right) Chuck beating himself up backstage. I could always count on Biscuits to be entertaining.

(above) John was dedicated to his instrument. I tried to capture him here, warming up backstage.

(left) On the road, you have to sleep when you can. After a long drive overnight, John takes a nap before the show.

(both pages) All photos by Jaye S. Clarke. I met Jaye twenty-two years ago in Columbus, Ohio. He first shot us at the Pterodactyl Club in North Carolina. As a friend I gave him unlimited access, and he shot us from 1988 through 1994. These are just a few of his amazing shots.

(below) While flying the friendly skies, Chuck has fun at the expense of a snoozing John Christ.

(below) The happy travelers are off on another trip to strange and exotic lands.

(left) John's guitar tech, Crash, took this one of me in Japan with all the guitars on my Christmas list.

(above) Glenn had been to Japan a few times on holiday and was happy to be going again. Chuck, not so much.

(above) John would practice before every gig, and then go over the show in his head afterwards to see where he made mistakes.

(left) Glenn and I went sightseeing in Japan; he took this one of me in front of one of many pagodas

Ocean Way, LA: 4p

I don't know whether Rick Rubin was just not as busy, or if he had renewed his interest in the band, but he was back in the studio wth us for *Danzig 4*. I think the success of the "Mother" single and video from the *Thrall: Demonsweatlive* EP might have been a factor. Grammy winner Jim Scott was at the helm as engineer for the sessions, and we worked at Ocean Way Recording in Hollywood. Jim is great to work with; very smart, very mellow, and he knows how to get a great drum sound. ▪ After the gold-record success of "Mother," I think Glenn deliberately wanted to go in a different direction. This was not a surprise to me. I don't think he ever really wanted to become too popular or lose his indie credibility. In my mind, *Danzig 4* was more of a Samhain record. It was more atmospheric,

and the songs were not as crafted in a classic sense. In other words, not every song needed to have the same structure: verse, chorus, verse, chorus, guitar solo, etc. ▪ John thought the material could have used more polish, but I felt the songs had a fresh feel. I was very happy with the vibe of the record. We recorded yet again in only one or two takes. A lot of Danzig fans were disappointed in the fact that there wasn't a hit single. However, considered within the overall body of work we had done to date, *Danzig 4* fits well with the other records from the period. ▪ Finally, as if to predict the future, the band was all photographed in coffins for the CD package. After all, this would be the last record with the four of us–the original lineup of Danzig.

(both pages) Rick Rubin and engineer
Jim Scott set up shop in Ocean Way
Recording's Studio A.

On The Road: 1994
Also featuring the
photography of Jaye S. Clarke

EERIE VON
"MORFIN"
IN TORONTO
94

2 DAT JAY GUY
JUNE 10TH
'94

(this page) Jaye took this photo of me on June 4, 1994 in Toronto, and Chuck Biscuits was inspired to draw this cartoon, which he later gave to Jaye. Pictured below is the artist at work.

DANZIG

summer '94

P

(opposite page, middle) Glenn got up and sang The Misfits song, "Last Caress," with Metallica on a few occasions. Chuck even got in to the act by playing one of James' Gibson Explorers. Over the years, Kirk and James, Glenn, and I would often get on stage together and play Misfits songs. I played bass or drums and it was always a blast. Photos by Jaye S. Clarke.

SH*T IN THE SHEDS '94

METALLICA

SPECIAL GUEST

DANZIG

+ SUICIDAL TENDENCIES

DES MOINES
IOWA
JUNE 25

SOMERSET
WISCONSIN
JUNE 26

JAM

PRODUCTION / FIELD
CREW STAFF

NOT GOOD FOR ADMISSION ON SHOW DAY

BRAND NEW GOD
SNAKES
COMIN DOWN
MOTHER
HOW THE GODS KILL
BLACK WINGS
TWIST OF CAIN
LONG WAY BACK

DEMON
DIRTY BLACK SUMM

(upper right) We played on
THE JON STEWART SHOW
twice, once each with Chuck
Biscuits and Joey Castillo.
Stewart liked the band
and treated us very well.
It was always fun to be on
television.

DANZIG ROOMING LIST

BAND

8 - SINGLES	ROOM#
VICTOR CREED	206
LEE MELONE	212
DON BODERME	202
PADDY O'FURNITURE	218
RICK DIESING	210
MIKE BALL (Bus Driver)	204
SECURITY	220
KENNY DIDIA (pays own)	208

(facing page) I didn't shoot our band too much on this tour, but I did manage to get a few shots. Being able to sit onstage and shoot was always a treat.

The I Don't Mind The Pain Videoshoot

(this page) Out in the desert on a location used in quite a few big Hollywood movies, we filmed the last video John Christ and I would do...

...with the band. "I Don't Mind the Pain" also marks the first appearance of our second drummer, Joey Castillo (left), who took over after Chuck's departure.

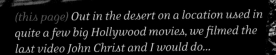

(opposite page) When the bus broke down in one-hundred-degree heat, a trusting real estate agent came to our aid and let us hang out in a model home until we could get transportation. I took these shots of the guys relaxing in this unnatural setting, including Glenn trying on my hat.

End of the Road '95

(right) With longtime friend and punk rock legend Brian Baker (from Minor Threat, Dag Nasty, Bad Religion, and very early Samhain).

(below, top) Dennis Keiffer, a kickboxing champion, took over security after Jesse James left. Here he helps Glenn with his daily workout.

(below, center) After John and I left, Joey Castillo remained with Glenn for years. Eventually, he left to join Queens of the Stone Age where he has been since.

(left and center) Mary Von, Sheri Moon Zombie, and Rob Zombie at Glamourcon in L.A. It's so sad when good people turn to porn...

(left and bottom) The band at the Rock Am Ring Festival in Germany, June 3rd.

(right) Rick Dittamo and me outside Zounds studio in New Jersey. Danzig rehearsed there in 1988 before the move to California. Most of the first album was written there.

(left) Mary Takes a tour of Manson's "Road Map of Scars." At our first gig together, the phone rang in the production office and John Christ happened to answer it. Someone from the Church of Satan was calling for Manson. What a way to start a tour!

DAN4ZIG
GOLDEN DOME   CITY PITTSBURGH
5.00
6.00   DATE 4/30
                        CURFEW
                   PERFORMANCE TIMES
KORN   7.00   TO   7.30
SET CHANGE   FROM 7.30 TO   7.45
MANSON   FROM 7.45 TO   8.30
SET CHANGE   FROM 8.30 TO   9.00
DAN4ZIG   FROM 9.00 TO 10.30
SHOW RUNNING TIME (APPROX)

(right) Manson ascends the stairs after being asked for an interview. He agreed to talk, but only if the writer, who was deathly afraid of heights, performed the interview at the very highest point at Sloss Furnaces. Hilarious!

(left) Twiggy Ramirez of Marilyn Manson at Sloss Furnaces in Birmingham, Alabama. He's not really sure which way is up.

151

(this page) Best buds, who just happened to be on the verge of becoming rock stars.

DANZIG
W/ MARILYN MANSON AND KORN
COUNT BASIE THEATRE
WEDNESDAY, APRIL 26, 1995
DINNER
POT ROAST WITH GRAVY
WHIPPED IDAHO POTATOES
HERBED CARROTS- STEAMED BROCCOLI
BLACK BEAN CHILI WITH RICE
CHEESECAKE
CHOCOLATE *DEVILS FOOD* CAKE
APPLE PIE ALA MODE

The End of an Era

Chuck Biscuits left the band after the Metallica tour, before the release of Danzig's fourth record. Certain promises were not kept, so he split. The only band he had stayed with longer than us had been D.O.A. Now we had to find a new drummer. No one could fill Chuck's shoes. We just had to get someone else and keep moving. We auditioned a bunch of guys, and the last one to try out was Joey Castillo. He had been in the punk band Wasted Youth, which gave him a leg up with Glenn. Joey was a nice guy who wouldn't make waves. He was young and eager He got the job. ■ John and I worked with Joey for about thirty days, then we went on the road to promote *Danzig 4.* Previously, we had the likes of Soundgarden, Type O Negative, C.O.C., and White Zombie opening for us. It seemed like most of these bands would surpass us in the years to come. This time we had two brand-new bands opening the shows: Korn and Marilyn Manson. Korn was what people were calling "nu metal." They played seven-stringed guitars, and had sort of a Latino gang vibe about them. They brought the younger crowd back out to see us. Marilyn Manson, whom I had met backstage after a NIN show, wanted to be weird, and tried to shock us every chance they got. They simply couldn't. Every single night with them was a rolling sexual circus full of drugs and debauchery with accomplices I dubbed the "Manson Girls." Even though I was only eight or nine years older than them, they called me "Uncle Eerie" and asked about the bands from the old days. They wanted to know what it was like to record on tape, and other historical stories from a bygone era! Korn and Marilyn Manson were both very entertaining, and they brought a much-needed spark of youthful energy to that leg of the tour. True to form, within the year both bands had left Danzig in the dust. ■ John had not been happy in the band for a long time. I think being the only metal guy, he felt like an outsider. Chuck and I knew John regarded the band as Glenn's band and not *our* band like it had been in the beginning. He was biding his time, making a name for himself until he eventually moved on. Well, that time had come. With Biscuits gone, a lot of the soul of the band was gone, too. I was going through my own personal stuff. My chronic back pain wasn't helping, but we forged on as best we could. ■ John decided he would finish whatever tour and video obligations remained. Then, after the South American leg, he would hand in his resignation. He even wrote the words I QUIT on the back of his guitar, so he could hold it up at the last show in Santiago, Chile. He never got the chance. The band and crew flew ahead to the final gig, but Glenn simply never showed. I don't know what happened, but the show was canceled. Regardless of anything else, John quit the band. Naturally, the prospect of going on tour and making records without my two good friends was simply not something I wanted to do. Therefore, I decided to leave as well. ■ I called Glenn from New Jersey and said I wasn't into doing this any more. It was a hard thing to do, but what made it worse was that Glenn didn't ask me to stay. He didn't bring up the twelve years of friendship and all the good times. He didn't thank me for the loyalty. Instead, he just said, *Call me if you need anything.* ■ So there you have it. What started after the breakup of the Misfits in 1983 had finally run its course after many records, tours of the world, ups and downs, and the whole ball of wax. It was a real rollercoaster ride, and I loved *nearly* every minute of it. I am very proud of the records we made, the millions of people we made happy, and the friends and lovers I met along the way. Yet the time had come for me to move on.

(left) We packed up our stuff for the long journey home, and nobody knew we had just played the final show for John Christ, Rick, and myself.

(above) 1. *DJ, Crash, and Morgan try to keep their jobs.* 2. *Randy Calloway (bus driver)* 3. *Dennis "The Cobra" Kieffer (total security)*
4. *Jeff "Jebbi" Kritz (monitors)* 5. *Mark Raoul Hall (bass)* 6. *Lance Eubanks (bass)* 7. *Jaye S. Clarke* 8. *Bob Montgomery (first drum tech) and Mitch Kramer (first bass tech)* 9. *DJ White (drums)* 10. *Yogi Garcia (drums)* 11. *Crash and John Araya*

Eerie Von & Mike Morance
Uneasy Listening
(1995, Caroline)

The Blood and the Body
(1998, Cleopatra)

Bad Dream No. 13
(2005, Ghastly)

Spidercider
(2006, Ghastly)

Kinda Country
(2009)

went back to New Jersey. Less than a year after leaving Danzig, I was living with Mary and working on my songwriting with Rick Dittamo back at Zounds rehearsal studio. There I found Mike Morance answering phones, booking bands, and taking care of things while Rick and I rehearsed. ■ Mike was a local underground legend who had been in bands during the first wave of punk. He put out solo records and would occasionally sit in on sessions with his friends. He didn't particularly want to work with anyone, as he didn't really like people. He mostly kept to himself and couldn't be pinned down. I liked that. I was already planning on doing a record. I thought I could get a deal on my name alone. I asked him if he'd be interested in working with me. He could have free rein, and I would give him half of whatever I could con out of a record company. To my surprise, he said *yes.* ■ I had three or four ideas on tape, a storyline, and that was about it. Mike had ten years' worth of stuff in his head. After the first day we left Reel Platinum with three songs. Mike couldn't believe it. Two sessions later, we had what I called *Uneasy Listening.* It was a spooky horror-movie soundtrack type of record where I imagined each track to be part of a film that didn't exist. I had dealt with Tom Bejgrowicz at Caroline Records when he asked me to write the liner notes for a Misfits box set. I called him, told him what I had, and he gave us a deal. We've been friends ever since. ■ I had been talking to Rob Zombie a lot, and some ideas were floating around about maybe working on something together. Mary and I decided to move back to L.A. to see what we could get going out there. I rented a single apartment on Coldwater Canyon and spent a year hanging out with Rob and his wife Sheri while working on my next record. I had a four-track recorder, acoustic guitar, microphone, distortion box, and a Casio keyboard from Toys "R" Us. Rob decided to break up White Zombie and do a solo record, so I figured I would get involved. It didn't happen. After a year, I had my next record *The Blood and the Body* ready to go. Mary and I found an 1877 Victorian house online, and decided to split for Florida. ■ We took a cross-country trip in my 1970s Olds Cutlass, with stops in Tupelo to see Elvis' birthplace and in Memphis for his big house. Somehow or another, I got Cleopatra Records to put out the new record. While I spent every nickel restoring the house, sweating my ass off down South, I looked for guys who wanted to play the blues. Mary and I got married, and our little town began hosting a motorcycle convention every year. We took a few trips to the Playboy Mansion for Mary, who had been modeling for them for years. Next up were a few hurricanes every season, a bunch of cats, and a new record. This is when I started painting

chapter 4

And Then There Was One....

1995-'09

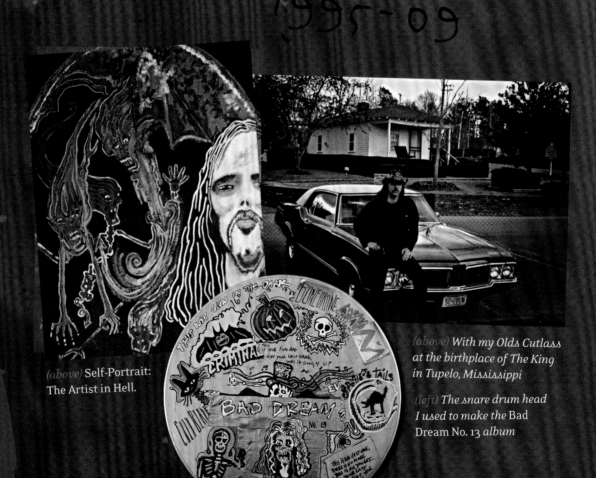

(above) Self-Portrait:
The Artist in Hell.

(above) With my Olds Cutlass
at the birthplace of The King
in Tupelo, Mississippi

(left) The snare drum head
I used to make the Bad
Dream No. 13 album

(below) With my family in New Jersey, 2006

CREEP SHOW
EERIE VON MELDS GOTH AND AMBIENT
MUSIC INTO UNEASY LISTENING.

(right) Meeting Butch Patrick, aka Eddie Munster, in Florida
(upper right) Tom Bejgrowicz and I having a beer at Poor
Richard's Pub in Scranton, PA. Photo by Jennifer Martin.

(above) Scranton,
Pennsylvania, July
2008. Photo by Tom
Bejgrowicz.

full time. To my pleasant surprise, people liked what I was doing, and I started auctioning them on eBay. ■ I recorded my third record, *Bad Dream No. 13*, on a steady diet of Jack Daniel's around 2000 in my toy room beneath the glow of black light and my vast collection of skulls and monster memorabilia. To pay the bills I sold off original photos and most of my record collection, except that I kept one copy of every Misfits release for sentimental reasons. At about this time, Bob from Rosemary's Babies decided he wanted to put out a CD for the 25th anniversary of the band. He revived Ghastly Records, our label from the old days to put out my *Bad Dream No. 13* record, too. So I remixed half by email, making extensive notes and corresponding back and forth with the engineer and Bob. Bob mastered it, and it came out great. ■ I went to work on my next project, *The Bastard Blues,* using my new digital recording system. Halfway through, the hard drive crashed and I lost a year's worth of work. I abandoned the project, and started working on demos for what would become *Spidercider.* Before I made any real progress, we decided to sell the Victorian house in Florida and move to Indiana to restore Mary's great-great-grandfather's house; a Civil War-era doctor's place on an acre-and-a-half in the middle of nowhere. Florida was too friggin' hot for me, and I never liked the sun. So why not? ■ Fairmount, Indiana, was James Dean's hometown. He's buried there, and they have a festival in his honor every year. That works for me.

The people were really nice, even a little too nice. I wasn't used to it. There were also cows, horses, and cornfields everywhere. I could have lived there forever. I was getting good money for the paintings, making contacts online, hoping something would come along so I could get back out on the road and get back into the big game. Somewhere along the way, things with Mary fell apart. We had been together since the Metallica tour in 1994. She left, and I dove headlong into the *Spidercider* record, writing and tracking at all hours of day and night. It was good therapy, and I was angry; that lent itself to the vibe of the record. When I was done, Bob said he would put that one out, too. I moved back to the East Coast to be near my family, whom I hadn't really seen much in ten years or so. ■ I was in pretty bad shape, but I kept painting and working on my songs. I managed to get fifteen to twenty tunes together in my first year back. I figured out how to record and paint in the daytime hours and wound up with my *Kinda Country* record. Alone again for the first time in fifteen years, I was free to get back on the road, and that's what I'm going to do. ■ This twenty-six-year career of mine has been a hell of a ride, but I keep right on going. When others have given up, I won't. This is what I do. After all this time, I can't change anyway. That's it, you're all caught up. Look for me in your town, or online, and pick up a painting, why don't you? Thanks for buying this book, and for reading my story. I hope to see you all real soon.

Fiend Art

(left) In the painting studio, 2008. Photo by Tom Bejgrowicz.

(right) Headcase.

(left) Masque

(right) Manmade.

(left) Magdalena.

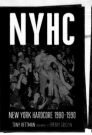    

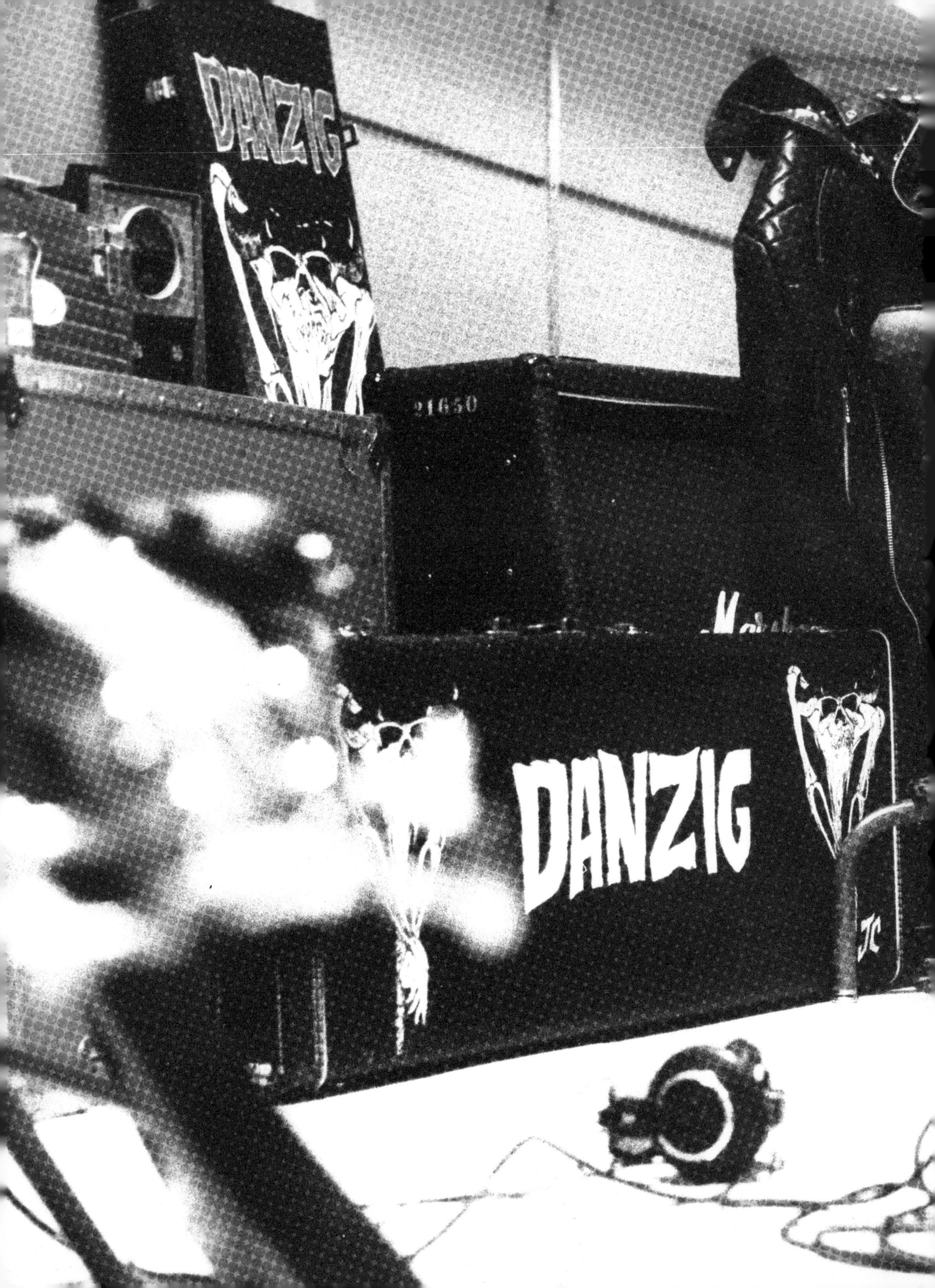
DANZIG
21650
DANZIG
JC